CHRISTIAN
FAMILIES
IN RECOVERY

A GUIDE FOR ADDICTION, RECOVERY & INTERVENTION
USING GOD'S TOOLS OF REDEMPTION

by Robert and Stephanie Tucker

Christian Families in Recovery
Written by Robert and Stephanie Tucker

Published by:
Spirit of Life Recovery Resources
18652 Florida Street, Suite 200
Huntington Beach, CA 92648

All monies from this book purchase will help accomplish our mission. Spirit of Life Recovery supports people struggling with emotional and spiritual challenges, including addiction and codependence. Spirit of Life Recovery is a 501 (c)(3) non-profit Christian Ministry— Fed tax #27-3278002. To learn more, visit www.spiritofliferecovery.com.

Editing services by ChristianEditingServices.com.

Unless otherwise indicated, all Scripture quotations are taken from the Holy Bible, New Living Translation, copyright 1996, 2004. Used by permission of Tyndale House Publishers, Inc., Wheaton, Illinois 60189. All rights reserved.

Scripture taken from The Message. Copyright © 1993, 1994, 1995, 1996, 2000, 2001, 2002. Used by permission of NavPress Publishing Group.

The stories and examples may or may not be based on actual clinical situations, however, where applicable, names were changed to protect privacy.

This book is not necessarily intended to diagnose or treat your individual issues. If you are in a serious or life threatening situation, please get professional help immediately. This book is in no means intended to replace the need for professional and/or medical treatment.

For grammar, editorial or any other issues pertaining to the quality of the production of this workbook, please contact the publisher, Spirit of Life Recovery, directly.

Printed in the United States of America

This book is dedicated to all family members of New Life Spirit Recovery—past, present and future. The heart of God is to restore relationships and families. May you abide in Him, seek Him, know Him and find He is above all circumstances, all human knowledge and all challenges that you face. Trust Him—the mighty I Am—to do for you what you cannot do for yourself.

Introduction

When people walk through the doors of New Life Spirit Recovery, the crisis of addiction is fresh. There is pain, anguish and confusion. The addict is oftentimes beat down, fearful of what lies ahead, and overwhelmed to face the path of destruction they had created. Some are ready for help. Others aren't.

The family members are desperate. They want freedom from the addiction cycle, but they are taking a risk. In some cases, everything is on the line: marriages, finances, jobs, children, the future. The thought of this being another dead end is almost more than they can bear.

Entering into people's lives at this point of crisis takes care, empathy and love. It also requires truth. Truth is at the foundation of all positive change and redemption. Both the addict and the family members want to believe that life can be better. They want to embrace the promises and truths they have been exposed to in their own Christian experience. But they don't even know where to begin.

If it could be visualized, the addiction cycle is like a hurricane that stormed through the family system and created wreckage and destruction for everyone involved. Its ferocious force stole what had been considered precious. In its pathway were not only the loss of dreams, but in many cases the loss of the God-given identity of each person involved. Addiction was no longer a mere unwelcome visitor, but now controlled the family like a dreaded slave master.

Like the aftermath of any storm site, reactions can come in varied ways: shock, denial, confusion, disconnection, anger and other coping mechanisms. If the addict partakes in a journey of recovery, the family is stuck dealing with the residue of the storm damage. They cannot move on as if nothing happened. If the addict relapses or remains in addiction, the family becomes hopeless and filled with despair.

It is our heartfelt belief that when the family understands the reality of what is happening from a biblical, spirit-led perspective, it can remove the insanity that addiction creates. Truth begins to act as a light, even when it is unpleasant to see. That's because truth provides a means to entering into the "clean up" phase. In darkness, confusion remains and overwhelms. But in the light not only can God begin to reveal what's broken, He can also begin to inject His very own resources.

Over the years we have developed resources to assist in individual recovery for everyone affected by the addiction cycle. But we weren't able to provide the necessary insight, education and support to show families what that actually entailed from beginning to end from both sides of the addiction.

We wrote this book to fill in the gaps of what occurs between crisis, intervention and recovery. The basic premise of this process is that family members are enlightened and validated in the addiction cycle, recognizing their own needs and setting healthy boundaries. So often we hear in recovery circles (and were guilty of saying ourselves) "everyone just needs to work on themselves right now." In many ways this is true and as you'll discover, this book will emphasize that. But the reality is that addiction was a family issue, it did disrupt relationships, and it needs to have a family-centered approach. God created the family system as the foundational institution of society. If it matters to Him, it must matter to us, too.

We wish we could tell you that there are quick and easy solutions to the dilemma of the addiction cycle. Honestly, we cannot. But we can introduce you to the way God is able to interject, sort, sift, bring understanding, offer hope and give direction to everyone involved.

As the authors of this material, we are motivated not by the latest breakthrough in science medicine. We are motivated by the One who contains all power in the Universe to overcome darkness. Jesus Christ bled on the cross not so we could rely on a healthcare system entirely to resolve the current power of addiction. Certainly, He does use medical professionals to assist. But Jesus died to give us life. He died to overcome the ferocious enemy of our souls and declare His "enoughness" by merit of grace. In a society that has all but rejected His role, this book seeks to give Him His rightful position. The process will introduce you to a God that has a "hands-on" relational style, and One that is intimately engaged in the process of healing.

Both our program and materials were birthed from personal pain, not merely professional expertise. We both (Robert and Stephanie) dealt with our own disaster scenes and maneuvered through unfathomable levels of chaos. *But then God came onto the storm scene.* Can we say that line one more time to emphasize its importance? *But then God came onto the storm scen*e. And that changed everything.

The God of the Bible isn't an idea, theology or story. He is a Father, Friend, Savior, Redeemer, Rescuer and Healer. The God we met we've now witnessed hundreds, perhaps thousands, of others meet in the same way.

Wherever your own storm has led, and however much it has brought destruction, it's not too big for God. When He comes to your storm site, He brings with Him supernatural resources that can do for you what you cannot do for yourself.

We can't promise you a certain result, but we can promise that as you learn to be embraced by your Father in Heaven, He will offer you sanity, peace and wisdom. You will be loved, understood and validated. And you will gain insight and tools to help you rebuild, restore and walk into His purposes for life and relationships.

If you are ready for a deeper personal healing, we have additional books that can help you. But more than anything, get connected in a community that can help and support you right now in your own situation.

We pray with you and consider it a sacred honor to speak into your life.

With His love and grace,

Robert and Stephanie Tucker
Directors of New Life Spirit Recovery & Spirit of Life Recovery
www.newlifespiritrecovery.com
www.christianfamiliesinrecovery.com
www.christiancodependence.org

Table of Contents

Chapter 1: Facing Addiction... Page 7

Chapter 2: Outward Addiction .... Page 15

Chapter 3: Inward Addiction .... Page 25

Chapter 4: Framing the Battle.. Page 33

Chapter 5: A Family Affair.. Page 39

Chapter 6: Surviving the Storm .... Page 53

Chapter 7: Intervention .... Page 63

Chapter 8: The Hope of Redemption .... Page 81

Chapter 9: Adjusting to Change... Page 99

Chapter 10: Freedom from Survival... Page 117

Chapter 11: Reconciliation .... Page 127

Chapter 12: Family Planning .... Page 141

Resources... Page 167

CHAPTER 1

Facing Addiction

Her voice was filled with desperation as she disclosed the baffling and chaotic five years that led up to her call. It was as if the blond-haired, blue-eyed, fun-loving boy she had raised was gone. In his place was someone driven by selfish and insane behaviors he used to maneuver his next high. From lying to ranting to manipulating to stealing, he was overtaken by a ferocious foe she had come to know as his addiction.

Rhonda was a hands-on Christian mother who encouraged her son Andy to be successful and happy. But despite her best efforts and deepest desire for his well-being, Rhonda couldn't overcome the problems Andy had faced. With an alcoholic husband and dad at the center of the family, Andy's basic need for fatherly love, modeling and discipline were not offered. Thus, Rhonda tried to fill in the gaps to make up for what her husband didn't live up to in Andy's life. She also took on an intense protective role with Andy to save him from further pain.

Rhonda loved Andy. She had been his biggest fan and encouragement to have a vision for his future. Andy started to drink socially like many high school students. He always convinced his mom he was "fine." Rhonda wanted to see the best in her son, so she didn't doubt the stories that excused his absence at home. Now she knows, much to her heartbreak, that everything he told her was filled with lies and half-truths that created an ideal far from reality. Andy had learned early on to take advantage of her love and gullibility toward him. He could tell her almost anything and she would believe him. He also knew he could ask for almost anything, and she would oblige.

The situation spiraled completely out of control when Andy was expelled from college and sought to build his life around friends and drugs. By now, Rhonda knew he needed help, but what kind of help was unclear. She had given her son money, bail, food, a car—the list never ended. Her efforts to love Andy in his addiction only seemed to make things worse, yet she felt left alone in fighting for his life because from her point of view he had given up. But the more she put into helping, begging, and bargaining with him to stop, the worse he got. In truth, Andy controlled Rhonda. And addiction controlled Andy. Thus, they were both insanely dragged into the addiction and shared the burden.

While her story was filled with unthinkable pain and chaos, it could have been told a thousand times before. Despite the unique situations and personalities brought into the cycle of addiction, once in full swing, addicts look much the same. They think and behave in similar ways, and the consequences lead them to jails, prisons, hospitals and the streets. At the very least, the addiction breaks relationships, a sense of integrity, future dreams and the ability to live within God's purposes. Society writes addicts off as hopeless. Churches do what they can, then accept that the addicts are "lost." Family and friends shrug and nod their heads in dismay.

Determined to Find a Solution

Rhonda's phone call may have echoed many that flood resource hotlines. But even though Andy looked like every other drug addict in America, *he was her precious son.* She had to combat the reality that she needed to save her son, but the horrific truth was she didn't know how. For Rhonda, the mishmash of information, advice and solutions for her son's problem left her with few answers but many different pathways. And each "professional" opinion seemed to contradict the last. Her confusion grew as she tried to sort and sift through what he needed. Did he have a medical problem? Was it entirely a spiritual need? Perhaps he was mentally ill? And by now she knew—despite what she'd been told—forcing him to a program didn't mean he would change.

Despite all she learned, Rhonda had yet to understand that addiction wasn't just stealing her son's life, but it was also stealing hers. Her life was consumed with Andy's needs and problems, and in the process, she had lost her own hopes and dreams. Rhonda didn't understand the nature of the battle Andy was engaged in, nor did she understand the enemy at work in his life. She was fighting a battle she had not been authorized or empowered to fight on her own, and was suffering devastating defeat as a result.

Both Rhonda and Andy needed help—desperately. Once Rhonda became equipped with the tools of recovery, she still could not save her son. But she stood the best chance of establishing an environment where God could intervene on her behalf.

And so, like anyone who has ventured on the journey of recovery, Rhonda began the journey to understand her son's addiction, while at the same time, understanding her own pain and heartbreak.

Is There Help?

No matter your relationship with addiction, this book is not a gimmick or quick fix. It doesn't slap a quick and easy solution onto a large and difficult dilemma. But it does provide the pathway someone like Rhonda needs to go on. And it is written for anyone who has ventured down that road and genuinely wants the help of the True God of the Universe. Our desire in presenting this workbook is to offer families a solution for understanding the problem and the cure of addiction by dealing with rooted issues. While some will argue there is never a cure, the sufficiency of the blood of Jesus opened the doorway for every area of sin and stronghold to be defeated.

This book is not being written through a scientific model and not based on specific research in any one area. We are not doctors, nor are we in any way trying to replace the need for medical assistance. Rather, this is the culmination of life experience, professional experience, education, evidence-based treatment, personal redemption and—most important—the unshakable, unchangeable Word of God. We have witnessed thousands of lives ravished by addiction and then brought back together through the resources of God. We've also, sadly, seen some people lose this battle. We don't say this to discourage or invoke fear—but to be *real.* Addiction is deadly. It's also lifelong—a commitment that far too many people in recovery take lightly.

Why Addiction?

No one aspires to be a drug addict. Andy didn't wake up one morning and decide to become hooked on drugs and alcohol. But he did initially make a choice to partake in the "fun" of partying. Andy most likely had no idea where the "innocence" of a high would lead. Addiction would become his best friend, the love of his life, and what he would serve and invest his future into.

But that was far from Andy's destiny. In truth, he wasn't "born that way." He was born with a purpose—an inner desire to find significance, acceptance and his own personal calling. Yet Andy, like every other human being, was consumed with the inward void of separation from God. Even though he was raised in a Christian family, there is a good chance that Andy didn't learn how to partake of intimacy with God. Without that filled or satisfied, he was left to try to fulfill his needs, desires and that gaping hole in his heart with something or someone else.

An Escape Route

But while his spiritual need was central, it also must be clear that Andy, and everyone else caught in addiction, has a *reason* for wanting to escape. In his case, Andy most likely had much disconnection and inability to express or feel emotions. With an alcoholic father, he had a critical relationship unavailable to him in many regards. But that's only one example. The reasons people are vulnerable to drug use can vary. At New Life Spirit Recovery treatment center, over 70 percent of program participants have dealt with a level of sexual assault. That statistic is astounding and can't be negated as contributing to the susceptibility to addiction. Abuse, trauma, neglect, unmet needs, or even peer rejection can all create fertile soil for the introduction of substance.

That's because the addict uses the "high" of addiction as a coping mechanism. It becomes a normal reaction to abnormal situations. Addictions are particularly attractive because of their ability to deliver false strength during times of challenge. However, this strength is a counterfeit of what God has to offer. There is a price to pay for these short-lived *moments of pleasure.* They are always followed by pain and suffering that eventually affects everyone and everything in their path.

Bob was only sixteen years old when he saw his cousin shoot heroin for the first time. He was horrified at this behavior and questioned the sanity of sticking a needle through one's skin. He also knew his cousin's life was filled with chaos. But only one short year later he was doing the same thing. In his rational thinking, Bob knew it wasn't logical or right to insert a drug-filled needle into his own body. But the conditions of his heart and life made pleasure and escape from pain utterly alluring. Bob was escaping life and pain—even though he was never in touch with that pain enough to understand it exactly. In fact, the frightened boy who wasn't comfortable in his own skin became extremely confident under the influence. It didn't take long for full-blown addiction to manifest.

It's easy to label the drug addict as a "bad" person. But anyone who has loved an addict understands that the *manifestation* of addiction is quite different from the *person* behind it. Andy and Bob were acting out from a compulsive obsession with drugs—to where their authentic personalities and identities were swallowed up by the addiction. Their entire lives became driven by chasing a high. People became merely a way to get that high. Not only that, the drug use stunted their emotional growth because it literally shut their emotions down. Did that make them bad people? In a behavioral sense, it was bad. Yet deep down, they were hurting kids who were lured to believe that drugs would resolve their inner conflict.

Addiction and Behavior

Separation of behavior from the person using drugs is one of the most fundamental principles in understanding addiction. While some see "bad," others only see the "good" side of the addict and excuse the behavior rather than confront it. In truth, the "bad" behaviors of addiction are nothing to condone or accept. In fact, the level of leeway the addict is given will determine how much the addiction affects those people around it. To clarify the impact in our own life experience, let's address this behavior and how we might have been affected. It's vital to *spend time* giving each area some thought.

Addicts carry common characteristics including the following:

- **The need to blame**—Addicts will relentlessly blame something or someone else as the reason they are using. This can include statements such as "you make me do this" or "I can't stop drinking when you're around." As long as a scapegoat is willing to accept that burden, the addict is perfectly justified in continuing.
  Do you ever feel blamed for someone's using? (If you are the addict, do you blame others?) If you take on that responsibility, how do you feel about it? What specific ways have you dealt with feeling responsible for their problem?

  _____

  _____

  _____

- **Serious denial of having a problem**—Addicts are unable to see the truth (this is called spiritual darkness), and can't understand how dysfunctional and hurtful their behavior is to all affected. Addicts are actually hurting themselves the most.
  Does the addict in your life deny having a problem? Do you believe this? If so, how does that make you feel? How do you specifically react to that denial?

_____

_____

- **Emotional and mental manipulation ("head games")**—Addicts will twist and warp the truth to make others carry their shame and guilt. In dealing with addicts, left is right, up is down, and black is white. Everything is distorted and twisted because their own minds are distorted and twisted because of the nature of addiction.
  Do you ever feel manipulated by the addict in your life? Explain some specific examples where truth has been changed. When you believe their "truth," how does that make you feel? How do you react specifically to this?

_____

_____

- **Manifestation of anger (through words or violence)**—Addicts can be very hostile, angry and abusive. The chemical is meant to numb their emotions, yet anger often manifests in even greater extremes.
  Are you confronted with anger or rage as a result of addiction? Explain how this looks. How has that made you feel? Explain your method to defend against it.

_____

_____

- **Chronic lying**—Addicts lie more than they tell the truth. Their entire world is a lie; thus they can't be trusted under the influence. Having a rational conversation with a drug addict or alcoholic under the influence of substance is absolutely impossible. This can be painful and feel like utter betrayal, but it truly is a *symptom* of the cycle of addiction.
  Are you exposed to chronic lying? Have you believed the addict's convincing stories in the past? How do you feel when you are being lied to? What have you done about the lies?

_____

_____

- **Defensiveness**—Addicts seek to protect themselves and their addiction. They will threaten anyone who opposes their next high. That's because the drug or alcohol high is like a passionate love affair. Anyone who comes too close will be dealt with through fierce jealousy.
  Have you ever found yourself competing with the drug? Did you ever feel if you confronted it "all hell might break loose"? How did you feel? How did you respond?

_____

_____

- **Immoral behaviors** (cheating, stealing, sexual, etc.)—While addiction isn't an excuse for immorality, it is bred directly in the addictive lifestyle. Thus, the natural fruit in an addict's life will be varying layers of immorality.
  Have you witnessed or been hurt by an addict's immoral choices? Did you ever feel it had

anything to do with you? What did you do about the behaviors?

_____

_____

_____

- **Secretiveness**—Addicts hide and keep secrets, mostly to protect themselves and their addiction.
  Are there secrets in your home? Do people openly communicate or hide? What do you feel about the "secret" mentality? How do you respond? Do you comply or resist the need to hide?

  _____

  _____

  _____

- **Isolation**—Many addicts end up living a very isolated life, where they are left alone with the love of their lives—the drug. The dependency is so great it actually competes with human relationships. In fact, human relationships are often used only to gain something that can help them get their next high.
  Is the addict isolated or alone? Are there stifled efforts to connect at a relational level? How does the addict's isolation make you feel? How do you typically respond to it?

  _____

  _____

  _____

- **Unavailability**—Addicts under the influence cannot be spiritually or emotionally available. Thus, all their relationships will be lacking in this area, even if they are physically present (which often they are not). An addict could even be described as a "shell of a person."
  Overall, do you feel the addict is unavailable? Does that unavailability affect you? What do you do to deal with that loss?

  _____

  _____

  _____

If you answered yes to even a few of these questions, you have been deeply wounded by an addict. Their addiction has had a direct influence on how you respond and live your life. Being under the influence of someone else's addiction is no small ordeal. *You must seek help.*

Please understand, if you hate the drug *addiction,* it's okay. If you are angry at the drug addiction, that's okay too. But the *person* and the *addiction* are two different things. As horrible as it is, that behavior has an influence and a reason. Once the influence is removed, that person has the opportunity to be someone altogether different. *People are not their addiction.* Others often fail to see this. Many times, Christians vacillate between tolerating the addict for a while, then simply casting them out. The purpose of this workbook is to do neither. Rather, it's vital we address addiction through God's perspective so we can wage war against the addiction—while seeking to restore the person.

We must also understand this will take time. If we think we can simply give an ultimatum that will prompt immediate change, we are not grasping the depth of the nature of addiction. Sobriety is the *beginning* of recovery, but it doesn't change the initial problems (such as seeking comfort) that caused the addiction. These underlying issues and triggers must be dealt with, or when the recovering addict stumbles upon them again, he will be prone to relapse.

To make better sense of addiction, picture a tree. The tree was planted as a seed (see Chapter 8). For the addict, that seed was often produced by neglect, abandonment, hurt, betrayal, lack of boundaries, feelings of worthlessness, rejection or lack of love. When seeds planted are based on lies (which are anything that contradicts God's truth), roots of addiction begin to form, and eventually the leaves and fruit of that seed are produced.

Addiction is merely external behavior that is the "fruit" in a person's "tree" of life. If the fruit is cut off but the root left intact, the addict will be "changed" for the moment, but that seed will eventually regenerate the "plant" of addiction and produce similar fruit. Removing the fruit alone won't change the production cycle! This is one reason people often switch addictions.

Recovery is about dealing with the seed and the roots. An addict will require an entirely new system change. In fact, all those "bad seeds" (lies) will need to be uprooted, and new seed sown in order to establish the production of God's fruit—fruit that leads to abundant life in Him.

Gaining God's Perspective

Addiction carries many definitions—from scientific interpretation to the issue of morality. Many people have their opinions on what it is and how it should be treated. All the while, the families affected by addiction are engaged in their own war zone, desperately looking for a way out. As a Christian family, we must ask this question: How does God view addiction?

When addiction enters the family system, it is devastating for everyone. But even in the darkest and lowest point, we are never beyond His grasp. As a Christian, you may know that as a truth, but embracing it as your actual reality is necessary for the power of God to be activated. That means it takes *faith* to believe that God holds the keys and answers to your life, including the person struggling with addiction.

This is very difficult to embrace because we have so much conflicting information in our culture about addiction. Not only that, but many of us have also been bewildered by the lack of success we may have witnessed through Christian disciplines. That's why we need to take the principles of addiction and recovery and place them under the filter of God's perspective. In fact, we must be willing, for a moment, to see this issue *not* through the scope of someone or something else but *purely* through the foundation of His truth.

What Would Jesus Do?

When Jesus walked this earth, He dealt with people with afflictions and problems of every magnitude. Within His own culture, He interacted with alcoholics and prostitutes, society's lowest and most mistrusted. This astounded and offended the religious people who held strict restrictions against any form of contact with such conditions. In our own culture, there can be a similar mind-set among Christian or religious people who say, "*Don't touch them.*" However, watching Jesus interact with these people gives us a glimpse into His heart. In truth, Jesus was unafraid and unaffected by the sin and sickness in the human. When He looked into the eyes of a broken soul, He saw His mission before Him. In fact, His purpose wasn't to judge sin but to provide a way of escape. Instead of pushing them away, He knelt down and met people at their point of need. He didn't give them a standard to reach, lessons to first learn or a physical prescription to adhere to. He simply did what He came to do—offer them a spiritual remedy that would provide access to a lifestyle of freedom. If they didn't want it, Jesus didn't coerce—nor did He condone.

Jesus was radical in warning of the devastating consequences of separation from God. He was also radical in declaring and manifesting the incredible benefit of believing in His name. That's because Jesus knew authoritatively that He possessed the power of God to fix, heal, redeem and restore humans. In fact, the Bible is packed with stories of Jesus engaging society's outcasts—those who were mentally, spiritually and physically broken. It was never of a matter of what He *could* do. Jesus knew exactly what He came to do. The choice always rested on the person who needed what Jesus offered. Those who received Him by faith gained access to His power. While Jesus sometimes healed people physically in an instant, most of their inward changes were just beginning. With a connection to God, they now possessed everything needed to be realigned physically, emotionally, mentally and spiritually. This is biblically known as *transformation.*

Two thousand years later, the epidemic of addiction is still rampant and the culture is swarming with people plagued by spiritual, emotional and mental maladies. With knowledge-based science, medical breakthroughs and more technology than people could have fathomed in biblical times, the problems haven't improved but worsened. Yet the source of power to heal and change the broken human hasn't changed. That's because that same Jesus is alive and well. And what He brought to earth through the gift of redemption *still* holds the necessary power to overcome the chains of addiction. If Jesus were to walk the earth, the question is, what would He do? How would He engage with those who are afflicted?

The nature of Jesus draws clear lines of choices. He is fierce in His warning and firm in His boundaries. But then He woos and draws people in by something even more intoxicating than a chemical—the authentic and powerful resource of His love.

Whether you or someone you love struggle with substance abuse, Jesus is the answer. He absolutely, undoubtedly can and will bring deliverance to the people who seek Him with all their heart. But He will not condone or allow the addict's lifestyle, nor will He intervene in the addict's life unless that help is requested. That's why your greatest weapon to free someone in bondage is to pray to the One who can deliver him or her. And for the person who is struggling, your greatest weapon is to call on the name of the Most High.

A Prayer of Deliverance
Lord God,
I invoke and invite you into the situation of addiction that has hurt me or someone I love. I have been deeply affected by addiction, and it has left deep and painful wounds inside my heart. Whether or not I have been able to express it, I admit it to you right now. I don't want to live under the influence of addiction. I want to help the addict (myself or someone else) but not in any way that will allow or condone the addiction. Oh Lord, help me! Help me to be free and able to be who you created me to be!
In Jesus' name, amen.

CHAPTER 2

Outward Addiction

It is vitally important that we embrace this journey by understanding what we have believed about addiction thus far. For most of us, receiving another injection of information may add to the already cluttered knowledge crammed into our heads. Others of us may be at the starting point. The first thing to understand about starting the journey of recovery is that we must gain *the mind of Christ* to lead us. If we have the attitude that addiction is merely a brain disease requiring a team of medical experts to help us unravel the mysteries, then our belief system empowers a medical solution. If we enter into this believing that the addict in our lives (ourselves or someone else) should simply stop, change, and live right overnight, we have imposed expectations that aren't possible apart from God's intervention. The addict cannot and will not change immediately.

Addiction is so baffling because it's not just a physical problem, nor is it exclusively a spiritual problem. It is a problem that affects the whole person—body, soul and spirit. Because each part is damaged and affected, the process of recovery requires attention in each area. But make no mistake—all recovery comes under the authority of God Almighty. As our Maker, Healer and Redeemer, He owns the formula to fix the human being that HE created from His own hand and heart.

Meditation Points:
What have I believed the problem of addiction stems from? What and whom have I believed can fix the problem?

Body, Soul and Spirit

In the next three chapters, we will look more deeply into addiction to get a better understanding of its origin. Also, by identifying the various components of addiction—physical, mental, emotional and behavioral—we can prepare to understand how intervention and recovery are intended to occur. Education alone can't change the heart. It is merely knowledge. However, the first step in moving toward a solution is receiving information based on truth. Let's take a deeper look.

The Body and Addiction

God designed our bodies with amazing processes. In His vast and incomprehensible design, He gave us systems that could sustain and carry out life functions. However, the reality of sin damaged God's design for our physical life. The same body created with glorious features now has a fallen and broken system operating at its core. The Bible refers to this as the flesh or the natural man. Not only is it broken, it was born separated (disconnected) from God.

Without a spiritual perspective of God as our Creator and sin as a human malady, we simply become material creatures left to be interpreted through a scientific model. We see this same mentality in understanding creation itself. When you take God out of the equation, you must find ways to account for life minus His power and ability. Much of modern-day science tries to explain both God-created functions and the fallen realities that occur as the result of mankind's sin. In both cases, science leaves wide and unanswered gaps—answers that can only be grasped through a spiritual understanding of people. While science can provide legitimate insight into how amazingly our bodies function (or malfunction), it does nothing to resolve the deepest need in each person's life—to be reestablished and brought into wholeness with God. That's because the body can operate without a spiritual connection, but it will have to manage and deal with a wide variety of deficiencies in the meantime. Humans are designed to be connected to God. Like an appliance without a power source, life without God can only be a shell not aligned with the purpose for which it was created—to love and worship our Creator. As healthy as the shell can become, it will still be fundamentally void.

Addiction Science

The science of addiction, in every sense of the word, is dealing with that physical shell. While the physical aspect can't explain the deeper roots of addiction, it is crucial because the body under the influence of addiction has malfunctioning processes occurring in the brain. As we study this, it's vital we understand that *true* science *is* God—not a replacement theory for Him. Science can't outsmart the One who created human life and everything in it. On the other side of the spectrum, simply ignoring the bodily functions leaves us lacking insight about the power of addiction.

Addiction and Neurotransmission

The brain is simply amazing. It houses billions of neurons (nerve cells) that send signals which are transported back and forth from one cell to another. These neurons send messages that provide the brain with information necessary to perform various functions. While the process is complex, basically the neurotransmitters are chemicals that carry messages from one cell to the next. Depending on their set task, these neurotransmitters can excite or depress the function of the neurons. For example, a neurotransmitter called dopamine releases a euphoric or pleasurable response. Its job is to tell the brain that something positive just occurred and should be repeated. Medical science calls this our reward system—it is linked to processes that drive us to "want more." Eating, for example, is driven by this system so that we will sustain life and nourish our bodies. Other neurotransmitters have different purposes and can activate areas of the brain associated with mood, emotion, and other feelings. Regarding the physical side of addiction, it is important to understand that these neurotransmitters are often the *physical* area where addiction takes hold.

We must keep in mind that the "reward system" of human beings is fundamentally driven by a fallen fleshly nature. The Bible repeatedly tells us to put away the lust of our flesh. Thus, the "pleasure" side of our lives can be misaligned without spiritual remedy. It is not that God doesn't want us to experience pleasure, but pleasure must be derived under His touch, not simply by our unchecked desires.

How Drugs Affect the Production of Neurotransmitters

Drugs are chemicals that can trick the body by either mimicking neurotransmitters or by causing them to flood the system. This creates an ultra-sense of euphoria. This alteration of neurotransmitter function creates a wave of problems. Because they are used excessively, the massive stimulation will drain the body's natural supply of neurotransmitters or cause the body to dramatically slow production. For example, introducing cocaine to the brain prompts the body to release a rush of the neurotransmitter dopamine, which gives the user a euphoric high. The rush of the drug, however, will eventually deplete the body's natural supply of dopamine and provoke a crash. The addict will then need greater doses of drugs to satisfy the depletion and to access a high. But satisfaction is *never attained* because the body has been tricked from its intended "normal" state. Thus, a vicious cycle is set in motion.

For example, Kimberly takes her first hit of cocaine and experiences a high. Her body responds positively at first and she is stimulated to want more. The normal function of her "reward system" is meant to urge her to repeat this activity. However, the drug alters this purpose and provokes an out-of-control cycle. As she continues to use cocaine, her body lessens production of its own supply of dopamine. Her body learns to adapt to the feeling the drug brings and begins to crave more. The more she uses the more her body adapts to that drug level. Then it takes more of the drug to satisfy her. Her brain is out of balance, and now it can't be satisfied by the compensating drug to get high. This is how a 20-year-old "nice girl next door" can become a prostitute or thief. It certainly isn't just a chemical issue, but the drug is an instrument from hell that places her into bondage. Her physical body is serving her cravings and addiction.

Now, Kimberly can't experience pleasure of *any* sort without the drug. Her body will become physically dependent on the drug and she will get sick without it in her system. Kimberly will also experience what are known as "cravings"—the very *thought* of the drug causes surges in brain chemistry that can drive her to insane efforts to find that "next high."

Understanding the science of addiction does not supersede the ability of God to bring healing. Yet, we must understand the power and grip it has on a person to lead them into a bondage where they lose the ability to make rational choices. Also, once addiction has altered the brain, it cannot be healed from a negative reaction to drugs. An addict's brain is permanently broken in its ability to say "stop." The moment substance is re-introduced to the brain, a person who had quit using is forced back under the compelling influence. This is also why it is not wise to "switch" chemicals. For instance, a person with a heroin addiction may justify using alcohol in its place. But because the brain is defective in its ability to say "no" this proves a very detrimental choice. In fact, the only way to assure true healing is never to use any chemical substance with a mind-altering effect; some prescription drugs may even be included in the mix and need strict oversight by a physician. While this is often questioned in terms of God's healing ability, it has been our experience that once a person is an addict, he or she should never pick up addictive drugs again. As we'll learn, this is not only linked to the physical body but has spiritual ramifications as well. This is why other activities, including eating, sex and gambling, can also become a source of addiction if not carefully monitored in recovery.

How Drugs Hurt the Body

We know the cycle of addiction leads to unthinkable chaos and shatters lives in unimaginable ways. In this chapter, we sought to understand the toxic effects of drug addiction solely in terms of how it harms the body. As we've learned, the brain is deeply impacted and led into bondage. However, the devastation of addiction doesn't end there. Different drugs erode different areas of the body such as the lungs, the heart and various internal organs. The purpose of this book is not to diagnose or give medical advice in any way. However, if you are dealing with a certain type of drug in your family member's addiction (or your own), it is wise to do specific research to understand the physical implications. Some drugs have a long-term impact on the body while others can lead to an immediate fatal overdose. Your research will help you gain a sense of the seriousness of the addict's condition.

Most people experience positive physical changes immediately upon detox, and the body will typically begin to heal in the absence of the drug. But this process can be painful and difficult. The brain may also be flat and dull without the drug's presence. *The addict will find it hard to adjust to a drug-free life without a spiritual remedy.*

Many programs treat addiction with other drugs to offset the uncomfortable periods of detox. Some Christians believe this is acceptable for a very short period of time, but ultimately the goal is for people to allow the Spirit of God into every area of their lives. In this chapter, we are only assessing the physical side of addiction. People who don't seek out the whole picture of addiction will usually stop right here and conclude that a medical solution alone must be sought. We want you to see the *entire* person suffering from addiction in order to assign a *total* solution.

Application Point:

To help you gain a perspective about your own situation, it is imperative that we link the physical side of addiction to the actual situation or person dealing with addiction.

Using the charts on page 19 and any research you have done on the drug you're aware of in the addict's life, write in this body outline (page 21) what may be some present symptoms and warnings. For example, a cocaine user may experience cardiac or cardiovascular complications, stroke or seizures. In black or blue, write out the symptoms that you have witnessed (or experienced). In red, highlight the potential dangers of those drugs and what may occur if continued.

Keep in mind, this book is not meant to replace a medical diagnosis of your needs. This is simply applying general and well-known information regarding addiction. *Please see a doctor immediately if you are suffering from any acute or long-term symptoms.* If you are related to someone with symptoms, you will have to determine the level of seriousness in terms of how or if you should perform intervention. We'll discuss this in detail in a later chapter.

Above all, remember that God is the Author of the human being and has a remedy to sustain and realign all things that are imbalanced or broken. He uses doctors and medical systems at times. At other times, He may simply transform the inner life and directly alter the physical body. He is the Author of life. Thus, in looking at the overwhelming nature of the science of addiction, don't get so lost in details that you forget to seek His face. He reigns!

Chart 1.1—Drugs, Effects and Health Risks

Drug	Street Name	Effects	Health Risks
Alcohol	Liquor, beer and wine	Low dose: Euphoria, relaxation, lowered inhibitions. High dose: drowsiness, slurred speech, nausea, emotional volatility, loss of coordination, visual distortions, impaired memory, sexual dysfunction, loss of consciousness	Increased risk of injuries, violence, fetal damage (in pregnant women); depression; neurologic deficits; hypertension; liver and heart disease; addiction; fatal overdose
Marijuana	Blunt, dope, ganja, grass, herb, joint, bud, Mary Jane, pot, reefer, green, trees, smoke, sinsemilla, skunk, weed	Euphoria; relaxation; slowed reaction time; distorted sensory perception; impaired balance and coordination; increased heart rate and appetite; impaired learning, memory; anxiety; panic attacks; psychosis	Cough, frequent respiratory infections; possible mental health decline; addiction
Heroin	*Diacetylmorphine:* smack, horse, brown sugar, dope, H, junk, skag, skunk, white horse, China white; cheese (with OTC cold medicine and antihistamine)	**Acute Effects**—Euphoria; drowsiness; impaired coordination; dizziness; confusion; nausea; sedation; feeling of heaviness in the body; slowed or arrested breathing	Constipation; endocarditis; hepatitis; HIV; addiction; fatal overdose

Drug	Street Name	Effects	Health Risks
Opium	*Laudanum, paregoric:* big O, black stuff, block, gum, hop	**Acute Effects**—Euphoria; drowsiness; impaired coordination; dizziness; confusion; nausea; sedation; feeling of heaviness in the body; slowed or arrested breathing	Constipation; endocarditis; hepatitis; HIV; addiction; fatal overdose
Cocaine	*Cocaine hydrochloride:* blow, bump, C, candy, Charlie, coke, crack, flake, rock, snow, toot	- Increased heart rate, blood pressure, body temperature, metabolism; feelings of exhilaration; increased energy, mental alertness; tremors; reduced appetite; irritability; anxiety; panic; paranoia; violent behavior; psychosis	Weight loss, insomnia; cardiac or cardiovascular complications; stroke; seizures; addiction; Nasal damage from snorting
Amphetamine	*Biphetamine, Dexedrine:* bennies, black beauties, crosses, hearts, LA turnaround, speed, truck drivers, uppers	- Increased heart rate, blood pressure, body temperature, metabolism; feelings of exhilaration; increased energy, mental alertness; tremors; reduced appetite; irritability; anxiety; panic; paranoia; violent behavior; psychosis	Weight loss, insomnia; cardiac or cardiovascular complications; stroke; seizures; addiction;
Methamphetamine	*Desoxyn:* meth, ice, crank, chalk, crystal, fire, glass, go fast, speed	- Increased heart rate, blood pressure, body temperature, metabolism; feelings of exhilaration; increased energy, mental alertness; tremors; reduced appetite; irritability; anxiety; panic; paranoia; violent behavior; psychosis	Weight loss, insomnia; cardiac or cardiovascular complications; stroke; seizures; addiction; Severe dental problems
PCP and analogs	*Phencyclidine:* angel dust, boat, hog, love boat, peace pill	Feelings of being separate from one's body and environment; impaired motor function;—Analgesia; psychosis; aggression; violence; slurred speech; loss of coordination; hallucinations	Anxiety; tremors; numbness; memory loss; nausea

Charting Addiction

_____

_____

_____

_____

_____

_____

_____

/21

Drug	Street Name	Effects	Health Risks
LSD	*Lysergic acid diethylamide:* acid, blotter, cubes, microdot yellow sunshine, blue heaven	Altered states of perception and feeling; hallucinations; nausea; increased body temperature, heart rate, blood pressure; loss of appetite; sweating; sleeplessness; numbness, dizziness, weakness, tremors; impulsive behavior; rapid shifts in emotion	Flashbacks, Hallucinogen Persisting Perception Disorder
Inhalants	*Solvents (paint thinners, gasoline, glues); gases (butane, propane, aerosol propellants, nitrous oxide); nitrites (isoamyl, isobutyl, cyclohexyl):* laughing gas, poppers, snappers, whippets	Stimulation; loss of inhibition; headache; nausea or vomiting; slurred speech; loss of motor coordination; wheezing	Cramps; muscle weakness; depression; memory impairment; damage to cardiovascular and nervous systems; unconsciousness; sudden death
Barbiturates	*Amytal, Nembutal, Seconal, Phenobarbital;* barbs, reds, red birds, phennies, tooies, yellows, yellow jackets	Sedation/drowsiness, reduced anxiety, feelings of well-being, lowered inhibitions, slurred speech, poor concentration, confusion, dizziness, impaired coordination and memory; euphoria, unusual excitement, fever, irritability/life-threatening withdrawal in chronic users	lowered blood pressure, slowed breathing, tolerance, withdrawal, addiction; increased risk of respiratory distress and death when combined with alcohol
Benzodiazepines	*Ativan, Halcion, Librium, Valium, Xanax;* candy, downers, sleeping pills, tranks	Sedation/drowsiness, reduced anxiety, feelings of well-being, lowered inhibitions, slurred speech, poor concentration, confusion, dizziness, impaired coordination and memory	lowered blood pressure, slowed breathing, tolerance, withdrawal, addiction; increased risk of respiratory distress and death when combined with alcohol
Sleep Medications	*Ambien (zolpidem), Sonata (zaleplon), Lunesta (eszopiclone);* forget-me pill, Mexican Valium, R2, Roche, roofies, roofinol, rope, rophies	Sedation/drowsiness, reduced anxiety, feelings of well-being, lowered inhibitions, slurred speech, poor concentration, confusion, dizziness, impaired coordination and memory	lowered blood pressure, slowed breathing, tolerance, withdrawal, addiction; increased risk of respiratory distress and death when combined with alcohol

Drug	Street Name	Effects	Health Risks
Codeine	*Empirin with Codeine, Fiorinal with Codeine, Robitussin A-C, Tylenol with Codeine;* Captain Cody, Cody, schoolboy; (with glutethimide: doors & fours, loads, pancakes and syrup)	Pain relief, euphoria, drowsiness, sedation, weakness, dizziness, nausea, impaired coordination, confusion, dry mouth, itching, sweating, clammy skin, constipation	slowed or arrested breathing, lowered pulse and blood pressure, tolerance, addiction, unconsciousness, coma, death; risk of death increased when combined with alcohol or other CNS depressants; less analgesia, sedation, and respiratory depression than morphine
Morphine	*Roxanol, Duramorph;* M, Miss Emma, monkey, white stuff	Pain relief, euphoria, drowsiness, sedation, weakness, dizziness, nausea, impaired coordination, confusion, dry mouth, itching, sweating, clammy skin, constipation	slowed or arrested breathing, lowered pulse and blood pressure, tolerance, addiction, unconsciousness, coma, death; risk of death increased when combined with alcohol or other CNS depressants
Methadone	*Methadose, Dolophine;* fizzies, amidone, (with MDMA: chocolate chip cookies)	Pain relief, euphoria, drowsiness, sedation, weakness, dizziness, nausea, impaired coordination, confusion, dry mouth, itching, sweating, clammy skin, constipation	slowed or arrested breathing, lowered pulse and blood pressure, tolerance, addiction, unconsciousness, coma, death; risk of death increased when combined with alcohol or other CNS depressants; used to treat opioid addiction and pain; significant overdose risk when used improperly
Fentanyl & analogs	*Actiq, Duragesic, Sublimaze;* Apache, China girl, China white, dance fever, friend, goodfella, jackpot, murder 8, TNT, Tango and Cash	Pain relief, euphoria, drowsiness, sedation, weakness, dizziness, nausea, impaired coordination, confusion, dry mouth, itching, sweating, clammy skin, constipation	slowed or arrested breathing, lowered pulse and blood pressure, tolerance, addiction, unconsciousness, coma, death; risk of death increased when combined with alcohol or other CNS depressants; **80–100 times more potent analgesic than morphine**
Other opioid pain relievers: Oxycodone HCL, Hydrocodone Bitartrate Hydromorphone, Oxymorphone, Meperidine, Propoxyphene	*Tylox, Oxycontin, Percodan, Percocet;* Oxy, O.C., oxycotton, oxycet, hillbilly heroin, percs *Vicodin, Lortab, Lorcet;* Vike, Watson-387 *Dilaudid;* juice, smack, D, footballs, dillies *Opana, Numporphan, Numorphone;* biscuits, blue heaven, blues, Mrs. O, octagons, stop signs, O bomb *Demerol, meperidine hydrochloride;* demmies, pain killer *Darvon, Darvocet*	Pain relief, euphoria, drowsiness, sedation, weakness, dizziness, nausea, impaired coordination, confusion, dry mouth, itching, sweating, clammy skin, constipation	slowed or arrested breathing, lowered pulse and blood pressure, tolerance, addiction, unconsciousness, coma, death; risk of death increased when combined with alcohol or other CNS depressants; muscle relaxation/twice as potent analgesic as morphine; high abuse potential

Drug	Street Name	Effects	Health Risks
Amphetamines	*Biphetamine, Dexedrine, Adderall;* bennies, black beauties, crosses, hearts, LA turnaround, speed, truck drivers, uppers	Feelings of exhilaration, increased energy, mental alertness;	increased heart rate, blood pressure, and metabolism, reduced appetite, weight loss, nervousness, insomnia, seizures, heart attack, stroke; rapid breathing, tremor, loss of coordination, irritability, anxiousness, restlessness/delirium, panic, paranoia, hallucinations, impulsive behavior, aggressiveness, tolerance, addiction
Methylphenidate	*Concerta, Ritalin;* JIF, MPH, R-ball, Skippy, the smart drug, vitamin R	Feelings of exhilaration, increased energy, mental alertness;	increased heart rate, blood pressure, and metabolism, reduced appetite, weight loss, nervousness, insomnia, seizures, heart attack, stroke; increase or decrease in blood pressure, digestive problems, loss of appetite, weight loss

Extracted from the National Institute on Drug Abuse Website. Used with permission.

CHAPTER 3

Inward Addiction

The reality of the outer body's addiction is extremely overwhelming. This alone can be enough to make us want addiction immediately removed. *If you are facing an urgent need or crisis, please seek help immediately!* But if you are just starting to research and understand addiction, it's vitally important to learn more about the inner working of a person's bondage. The physical body is not its own entity. It is linked to and houses entire processes that can be fed either by Spirit life or by the flesh. Apart from God, the addicted human only has the resources medical science can offer. But as children of God, we have access to the Healer and the One who can realign our lives from the inside out.

Soul Life

Throughout the Scriptures, the soul refers to our inner lives—how we think, feel and make choices (mind, emotions and will). It also entails our unique personalities and the detailed and intricate ways we are given a personal identity. We know from the Word that the soul is the eternal part of us. The physical life ceases; the soul lives throughout eternity. With this concept in mind, our faith and belief in God's truth must prevail over scientific and material-based thinking. Science simply cannot affirm or understand the unseen realm. When we step out of tangible realities and into faith-based spiritual principles, we must have the Holy Spirit living in us to be able to comprehend truth. Let's see what the Word says:

> But people who aren't spiritual can't receive these truths from God's Spirit. It all sounds foolish to them and they can't understand it, for only those who are spiritual can understand what the Spirit means. (1 Corinthians 2:14)

If we accept a scientific understanding of addiction (which is easy to do based on the tangible nature of addiction) but negate the Christian worldview, we too will be limited to the few benefits a medical community can offer. But as God's children, this should never be the case. God is all-powerful and while He can certainly manage the processes of the brain and body, He *also* has the power to remove addiction on the nonphysical level—to change the heart and set a person free internally. This freedom entails a transformation process in which the body, soul and spirit are each realigned and brought back to the purposes of God.

To gain access into the recovery and healing process, we need to understand the purpose and function within our souls in greater detail. Let's look at each part of the soul: the will, mind and emotions.

Will

The *American Heritage Dictionary* defines the will as "the mental faculty by which one deliberately chooses or decides upon a course of action." The decisions we make throughout life are filtered through our wills. God gave all people a *free will*, allowing each of us to choose how we want to think, respond and behave in a given situation. When the will is exercised and a choice is made, the outcome will be defined by what or who influenced the will in that situation. All choices of the will are fed by either truth or lies. When we submit to God's will, we become aligned to His purposes. But when we submit to lies, we come in agreement with Satan's system. This doesn't make a person satanic, but it does mean he or she is being deceived.

Before addiction took hold, the addict had choices. As the addictive drive took over, those choices were no longer available. Sin, and especially addiction, leads to bondage because it destroys the free will and places itself as the slave master. Thus, the free will is held captive, and the addiction itself is served. Many Christians don't understand the nature of bondage and become puzzled by the addict's choices. They think the addict should just be able to make wise choices and stop the insanity. However, because the will is so overcome by the addictive cycle, it will require a severing of that faulty and toxic influence and a re-attachment of the power source of the Holy Spirit (see next chapter). Without the Lord, it is beyond the scope of a human being to make this occur.

By understanding that the addict's will is held in bondage, we will be prepared to formulate proper expectations and also use God's tools of intervention (Chapter 7). While we are often alarmed and frightened by the addict's choices, God is not even slightly alarmed. He knows the power addiction contains. He also knows that He stands authoritatively above that power and can overcome its force. As we will learn, the way to help addicts is therefore not to *force choices* on their behalf but to allow the *Holy Spirit* to work in their life. Only He can remove them from bondage and lead them into truth. No human being can do this on behalf of another; it must be a personal choice of the addict's own will driven by the power of the Holy Spirit. This, in essence, can allow the will to be set free and aligned to make the right choices.

Mind

While the will makes choices, it bases those choices on the data it receives. This information comes from a wide variety of sources, including the senses, outside information, family influence, internal belief systems, God's Word and even such outlets as the media. This data may be helpful, informative and based on truth. Or it may be corrupt information somewhat like a computer virus that actually makes the mind sick.

The mind is where information is processed. It must not be confused with the physical brain—they are not the same thing. To help make better sense of this, let's break it down.

The Role of the Brain

Just as a computer has hardware, software and data, our brains function much like the hardware. The brain—meaning the actual piece of flesh functioning inside our physical body—is linked to the mind, but it does not have the same function. It is simply the infrastructure that provides a central "command" station (like the physical machine of a computer). The brain houses a variety of chemical processes that communicate information back and forth to the mind. We learned about the process of addiction as it occurs in the brain in Chapter 2. Because the brain is attached to our physical bodies, it will not last forever.

The Role of the Mind

The mind is much like a software program that sifts, sorts, categorizes and processes information for various uses throughout the day. While the brain is tangible (seen), the mind is intangible (cannot be seen). Because it is housed in our souls, the mind will continue throughout eternity. Therefore, our mind will be brought with us into heaven and be made whole and complete.

As Christians we believe the mind is either influenced by truth or held in bondage by lies. As we already learned, we have been given a free will. We have a choice in what we house in our minds. In fact, all data must pass through the "gate" of the free will where information is acted upon or rejected. For example, Mary receives a knock on her door. First, she must choose whether or not to respond to it. As she opens the door, she is flooded by a salesperson's pitch to buy a product. He uses many schemes to engage her in conversation, including flattery, fear and other manipulative strategies to influence her to buy a product. Now Mary is faced with another decision. Should she receive that data (sales pitch) and give it thought and consideration? Or should she simply slam the door? As Mary moves through the sales process, she is influenced and takes action to buy his product. Let's imagine the salesperson is a scam artist. The information Mary was given was false. But she believed what he said was the truth and gave him several hundred of dollars in response. She was now the victim of theft. The salesperson's fraudulent behavior was not Mary's *fault*, but she became *vulnerable* to his influence when she participated in the conversation. From that first knock on the door, Mary was dealing with data and processing it in her mind.

We experience the same process throughout our days. Our minds are constantly receiving and processing data. God's truth is attempting to align us with His point of view in all scenarios. This truth is given to us through the Word of God, Bible teaching and the overall influence of the Holy Spirit. The devil, like a scam artist, attempts to manipulate truth and deceive us so that we believe his lies. When he succeeds, he will essentially "rip us off."

This is an alarming reality because it is happening constantly, and we often don't consciously realize it. From the information we receive as truth, we form beliefs that eventually develop into an entire belief *system*. These beliefs drive every aspect of our lives. For example, terrorists believe that performing suicide bombings will earn them a lucrative position in "heaven." This belief drives them to pursue an insane and murderous agenda. The power of that belief cannot be minimized. Their beliefs lead to unimaginable consequences. While our belief systems most likely contain nothing that extreme, we can still begin housing faulty beliefs. And what we believe will affect how we think, feel and respond to both new and reoccurring situations.

Automatic Response

Not only are beliefs powerful, but when they become recognizable, our minds can instantly recollect something we've previously learned. This means we don't need to relearn the same things each day. The moment we see a chair, we know we can sit on it. We don't have to process long to recall that belief. It speeds down the path of a sort of superhighway that lets us react almost instantly. Using the previous example, when Mary is scammed by a salesperson, she will recall that situation whenever a sales process is initiated again. In some ways, this is good. This memory will protect her from future scams. But if it drives an ultra-sense of fear and scepticism (a belief that *everyone* will hurt her or rip her off), Mary may have trouble trusting anyone again. This has the potential to be toxic.

When the beliefs fed into our minds are true and accurate, they can help us become more functional, mature persons. We can build on acquired information and get smarter and wiser over time. However, when that data is *not* based on truth, the same mind created to help us can hurt us.

Lies can creep into massive areas of our lives and deposit deep-seated levels of shame and pain. For example, little eight-year-old Johnny repeatedly heard the words "you'll never amount to anything" whenever his father was disappointed with him. He heard his father speak those words over and over again. Rather than receiving help and encouragement, Johnny received a message of hopelessness that he eventually believed. He developed a *what's-the-use-of-trying* attitude.

As a child, Johnny believed whatever he was taught. The belief that he would never amount to anything was reinforced by his own will as he received (let in) this lie as truth. This negatively affected his perception of himself and others. Eventually, Johnny "checked out" of life and began the devastating road of addiction. Addiction led him on the pathway to insanity, and he, in essence, became exactly what his dad said he would become. It's not that his father knew this would happen. But a seed (based on a lie) had rooted, and that belief system took on its own form. Johnny's mind would be held in bondage until he could form a new way of thinking about God, himself and others.

These lies are also known as *unhealthy strongholds*. Most human beings carry some form of these strongholds because we live in a culture flooded by lies. In recovery, strongholds must be faced, understood and uprooted for the mind to be able to be brought into alignment with God's intended purposes.

What We Should Know

Studying the brain (the shell) may have some benefits, but we will quickly get overwhelmed by the technical knowledge it contains. As Christians, we need to be concerned with how the Bible instructs us on matters of the heart. The Bible makes no mention of the brain, but it references the mind over eight hundred times! That is not to say brain disorders, chemical imbalances and other problems aren't real. There are organic issues that may need the assistance of a physical doctor. However, for the most part, God deals with and heals the area of the mind, and the result is long lasting and true transformation.

In fact, the primary goal of the Christian life is to "renew our minds" and receive the "mind of Christ." Being transformed so we think like God thinks (Romans 12:2) is a process. We will cover this in great detail in future chapters.

Emotions

Emotions are an automatic response to the information processed in the mind. While thoughts at one point in time carried a choice, emotions are entirely different. They are the actual by-products of thoughts and produce an emotional reaction that is not based on a choice. For example, the windfall of a job promotion would instantly lead to a feeling of happiness and excitement. But the news of being fired would produce feelings of sadness and despair. Whether good or bad data is received, the emotions are not the actual problem; they are an automatic response to that information. In fact, they allow us to experience and express different feelings. Without emotions we would be nothing more than robots or appliances. Emotions are a God-given method to express our heart and to deal with what is occurring in our life. Unfortunately, if the information received is untrue, the resulting emotions can move a person to react unnecessarily and most likely in the wrong way.

In the case of the addict, his or her emotional system becomes extremely skewed. The addict has learned to avoid pain and not process it effectively, opting to medicate emotions rather than address the source. This means any pain felt as a result of data (information) is pushed aside, and the alcohol or drug becomes a quick fix to overcome that pain. While this seemingly alleviates the problem, it has a very distinct and unhealthy consequence—it removes the *benefit* of pain.

The thought of pain can warn us to defend against things that could permanently harm us. In fact, pain is often what keeps us from foolish and potentially dangerous activities. We use a knife carefully so we don't cut a finger. We avoid sticking a hand through a glass window because we don't want to be cut. Not only does pain help us avoid bad situations, but it also helps us seek healing. In the physical body, pain drives us to take action. If we are bleeding and hurting, we jump into action to get our injury stabilized. Our body even produces its own pain-fighting chemicals to assist us in the process.

The complete absence of pain would actually be dangerous in the case of injury unless we are so badly wounded we cannot help ourselves. With enough trauma, the body will naturally shut down to use the fewest resources. But when injuries are not at that extreme level, they throw us into survival mode so we will seek to fix the problem. Thus, in our daily lives, feeling pain is actually a good thing.

There are rare medical conditions in which people cannot feel physical pain. Because this so deeply damages that person's perceptions of danger and consequences, he or she can wind up with terrible, unidentified injuries or illnesses that can lead to infection or death. What seems like a gift—the absence of pain—actually removes a natural system of protection.

In the same way, our emotional pain is designed to signal what is happening internally. It is in every sense of the word an alert system. The experience of pain indicates there is something in us that needs to be addressed. While pain is never comfortable, it is intended to make us seek a solution. Because God is the Owner of our souls, He is in the only One capable of fixing their brokenness. He allows human beings to feel pain in a world that is fundamentally corrupt to protect them from the dangers that lurk and to remind them of their utter need to depend on Him and to receive, healing and comfort from Him. It's not that God wants pain to exist, but it is a natural consequence of this world's fallen condition. He intends for us to learn to use pain to teach us healthy survival. That's why feeling pain is not removed from the child of God. At the same time, that pain has a healing source—God Himself. Like ointment on an infected wound, He comes to address the very thing that has sabotaged our souls.

The drug addict has disrupted the very purpose of pain. Rather than feel it and face it—and thus identify its potential danger—the addict has learned to become emotionally numb. Not only that, but the addict's "reward system" is sabotaged. They momentarily feel good feelings by taking the drug and the body and emotions respond pleasurably. But because this distorts the system and deeply alters the purpose of God's distinct design for pleasure and pain (rewards and consequences), the addict is in an insane and self-destructive pattern of chaos.

The numbing of pain makes dangerous things seem nonthreatening. There are no natural consequences to guard against wrong choices when pain is removed. Not only that, but there is also no motivation to fix what's broken; there seems to be no need to turn to God. Instead, the false comfort of the drug cuts the addict off from reality and places him or her in danger. False pleasure creates a perverted illusion of what constitutes "feeling good." The addict reinforces the addiction and kills the opportunity to allow pain to motivate change. *This important dynamic is also critical for the family to understand.*

Emotions must be restored to their rightful place for the addict to heal because the emotional life has been deeply damaged. The addict is emotionally stunted and has no awareness of the actual God-given purpose of emotions. Thus, he or she has learned not to feel or process at all.

Ironically, in recovery, emotional pain must be felt and validated—not ignored. But emotions alone are not the root problem. They are the *symptom* of what is wrong. Just as a gaping cut produces pain, the actual *injury* of the heart needs to be validated in its source. The mind has to be understood and events, trauma, neglect, rejection, fear, and other feelings have to be processed.

God doesn't just remove pain. He returns pain to its original purpose—to reveal the problem. In recovery, dealing with emotions will center on the stabilizing of belief systems, where both pain and God's redemption will be seen in their proper perspective. When injuries of the heart occurred because of pain and violations of others, God will have to lead the addict through those offenses so he or she can be offered a spiritual remedy. Facing truth, however, will never mean that pain will go away. In fact, addicts will be asked to face the pain they couldn't deal with before they sought comfort in the bottle, pill or needle. Emotional healing will occur when they are allowed to *experience* feelings, grieve and rely on the comfort of the Holy Spirit. Maturity and emotional growth will begin at whatever level the addict "checked out" through drugs. Thus, a child who begins to medicate with drugs will have stopped learning to process emotions at that level of maturity.

In truth, only by feeling pain can the true remedy be prescribed. This is a key aspect in recovery and can't be bypassed, as emotions are always the area of deepest vulnerability. We'll discuss this in greater detail later on.

Preparing for Solution

Understanding the inner workings of the addiction itself helps us clearly see that trying to force behavioral change will not work! In fact, behaviors merely represent deeper problems. The nature of Christ-centered recovery injects the power of God through the Holy Spirit into the very places of dysfunction. As we will learn, this means the Holy Spirit has the resources to reverse addiction's effects and restore a person to wholeness. All this can occur when we learn to fight this battle as a spiritual war, not merely a physical, mental or emotional problem. We will consider this in the next chapter.

A Prayer to Understand

Lord God,

Grant me the ability to understand the magnificent way I have been created. Help me also to understand the addict in my life so that I can recognize there are deeper things happening than meet the eye. Prepare and equip me so that I may know how to serve You in this situation right now.

 In Jesus' name, amen.

CHAPTER 4

Framing the Battle

Hopefully by now you understand that addiction is a form of *enslavement*. Watching a person serve the enemy of addiction is unthinkable. And finding a true solution requires an aggressive look at what is essential to overcome the sheer force and power of addiction. For Christians, there is a time and place for practical wisdom and understanding regarding addiction. There is a need to know the physiological realities of addiction. There is also importance in understanding that the soul is sick and under addiction's toxic influence. With that background in place, we must be willing to unveil the rampant force of the *spiritual* drive of addiction. Even as we understand the battle of the body and soul, *true addiction originates in the spiritual realm and is authored by Satan.* The Bible says, "The thief's purpose is to steal and kill and destroy. My purpose is to give them a rich and satisfying life" (John 10:10). Brokenness and destruction are the reality of life apart from God. Addiction is a very obvious pattern of damage and death. Everything in the addict's life is wrecked, including health, emotional wellness, relationships, dreams, ambitions and hope.

Yet no matter how far an addict falls, he or she is never beyond God's grip. The character and purposes of God are redemptive in nature—they are to bring *life.* In fact, everything under the destructive force of addiction and then touched by God can be reversed and brought into alignment and wholeness in Him. We'll begin to address the process of recovery in Chapter 8. But for now, it's central to know that Jesus conquered sin and death—including addiction. And this is not merely Christian rhetoric. The reality is that He authoritatively sits above the forces of darkness. But the key to accessing this freedom is produced under very specific circumstances: the deliberate choice to let God have His way.

Before we can understand the magnitude of this reality and how God's intervention occurs, we first must prepare to understand the nature of the battle and the character of the enemy.

The Real Enemy

By now, hopefully, you can see that addiction is not merely willful sin and disobedience, but *bondage*. As we learned, this means addiction is holding the person in captivity. While the addiction itself seemingly overtakes a person's life, addiction is actually being influenced by a spiritual force. Satan is the enemy of the human race. He sets forth to oppress and sabotage people's minds so they cannot know God, experience freedom and live out the radical promises of what God offers. Satan is a fierce, bloodthirsty opponent who strategically develops ways to lure humans into his devices. Without identifying his tactics or acknowledging his role in addiction, we will be ignorant and prone to defeat. We will also be more willing to label addiction as merely a physical or emotional problem and thus limit the actual remedy.

Satan is behind the forces of addiction, but he doesn't parade around with fangs or horns making himself obvious. Satan, our enemy, actually attacks us in three different ways.

Enemy One: The flesh (sinful nature). We've already learned that our broken flesh is part of the corrupt system dominated by Satan. This doesn't mean we are actually *possessed*, but it does mean our bodies are fundamentally operating under that sick, sinful system (see Chapter 2). This is true for believers as well as unbelievers. All malfunctions of the body steal God's gift of life and turn it into an instrument of death. In addiction, the body is under the influence of its own broken condition. Without a spiritual remedy, this reality is dim for the addict. However, as Christians we have access to the Holy Spirit. As we'll learn later, the addict—and *all* Christians—will need to be conquered by the Holy Spirit.

> But there is another power within me that is at war with my mind. This power makes me a slave to the sin that is still within me. Oh, what a miserable person I am! Who will free me from this life that is dominated by sin and death? (Romans 7: 23–24)

Enemy Two: The world. The world, meaning the *system* of the world, fundamentally opposes God. Our current culture has all but kicked Him out of the public square, while welcoming and embracing principles and so-called "truths" that oppose Him. Thus, the world *system* (not referring to all the people, but to the overall mind-set, attitude and beliefs) is an enemy of God. When we are surrounded by a culture seduced by lies, it is very hard to live in truth ourselves. We must make a diligent commitment to know exactly what God's Word says and stay firm in believing His promises. Knowing what is real exposes lies. When bankers are taught to find fraudulent bills, they don't study the many counterfeit versions. Instead, they intensely study the authentic bills so they will easily spot one that is amiss. That's how it is with the Word. Obviously, this is an area of much vulnerability.

> For the world offers only a craving for physical pleasure, a craving for everything we see, and pride in our achievements and possessions. These are not from the Father, but are from this world. (1 John 2:16)

Enemy Three: Satan and his demons. As uncomfortable as the reality of an actual demonic realm may be, we are told in the Word that demonic activity is taking place. Satan and his army of demons function with strategies much like a physical war game. He works through people just as God works through people. He gains access into people's lives through their belief system and thought life, which can affect their feelings and overtake their will (choices). The baseline of everything he does is to lie and blind people from God's truth. The Enemy gains legal rights through sin-induced behaviors, and even from the generational curses of the family line. An actual deliverance prayer is strongly recommended as part of the recovery process. This can cut off any ties, connections or gained legal rights in the demonic realm. However, this must be done in conjunction with forgiveness and a submission to God. Forgiveness is the most powerful weapon against the enemy's tactics. Please note that while it's not wise to overly focus on the demonic, it is absolutely foolish to act as though it is irrelevant.

Let's read what God's Word says about Satan's role:

> Satan, who is the god of this world, has blinded the minds of those who don't believe. They are unable to see the glorious light of the Good News. They don't understand this message about the glory of Christ, who is the exact likeness of God. (2 Corinthians 4:4)

> For we are not fighting against flesh-and-blood enemies, but against evil rulers and authorities of the unseen world, against mighty powers in this dark world, and against evil spirits in the heavenly places. (Ephesians 6:12)

> You used to live in sin, just like the rest of the world, obeying the devil—the commander of the powers in the unseen world. He is the spirit at work in the hearts of those who refuse to obey God. (Ephesians 2:2)

Seduction

The formation of *all* sin comes through a seducing lie. The difference with the drug addict is that the stronghold of addiction can cause a physiological addiction and changes in brain chemistry that make it *very* difficult to combat. In fact, the moment chemicals trigger the brain's reaction, the vicious cycle quickly spins out of control. At least it does in many persons. Why some people are biologically prone to the "brain-chemical" trap of addiction—while others seemingly aren't—isn't something we can answer directly. But the motivation to find pleasure or remove pain is normally the drive behind substance abuse. And that's where we should focus. It's also important to note that there are many other ways we can seek to find pleasure or to remove pain other than chemical use. People use food, relationships, sex, work and many other vehicles in the same manner.

In essence, the seductive allure of addiction is the instant gratification of false comfort, happiness and power. What they deliver is short-lived. They are empty counterfeits based on a lie that stands in direct opposition to the true good which God provides. Not only are they void of delivering long-term solutions, but once a person takes the bait and falls into the trap, Satan delivers *exactly the opposite.* All his offerings lead to devastation, pain and loss.

A biblical example of this occurred in the Garden of Eden. God had provided Adam and Eve with absolutely everything necessary to be happy, fulfilled and blessed. But He required that they obey Him and listen to Him as the voice of authority. He warned them of a forbidden tree in the garden, saying if they partook of its fruit, they would surely die. After God's warning, Satan appeared to Adam and Eve in the form of serpent. At that point in history, it probably wasn't shocking to hear a snake talk. If they had thought this bizarre, or if Satan appeared with horns and a pitchfork, surely they would have fled the scene. But instead, this snake had a seductive way of offering them seemingly *something more* than what God had to give. Not only that, but the snake also distinctly claimed that God had lied to them and that they could attain something better if they ate from the very tree God was trying to deny them. As the historical account says, Adam and Eve took the bait because of their desire for that *something more,* a deeper knowledge than what God authorized them to have. And as a result, they were ensnared in a trap of death. They rejected the authority of God and thus empowered Satan's system.

While that may seem to be an ancient and impractical story, it couldn't be any more relevant in understanding the enticement of Satan. He works through the exact same strategy—luring people in with his lies and promises and then hammering them with the devastation of what that choice brings. He then drags them away to his authority system—where guilt, shame and fear prevail.

Can a Christian be an Addict?

Many people believe and even teach others that a Christian cannot be an addict. They claim people who live with such rebellion and immorality couldn't possibly have ever given their life to Jesus. While it's always possible that a professing believer didn't make an authentic conversion of faith, many times that simply isn't the case. That's because the powerful attraction of addiction is the lure—the seduction of the lie. If Adam and Eve in a state of perfection could be seduced, surely God's children can be as well. At New Life Spirit Recovery, many of our clients enter the program as Christians. In fact, we often have pastors, ministry leaders and teachers of the Word who love and have served God, yet fell into the chains of addiction. They had areas of vulnerability and weakness. The enemy promised the alluring something more, using strategic methods that directly competed against God. The moment these believers stopped seeking God for their comfort, power and needs and chose to believe that a substance could deliver those things instead, they were tricked. In essence, they "ate the apple," something attractive that could deliver momentary pleasure but later resulted in massive and horrible consequences.

Because the behavior of an addict is so negative, it's easy to believe they must not really know the Lord. However, that person, even a child of God, is influenced by a system rooted in the kingdom of hell, and the effects of their lives look as such. When the person is brought back, he or she will be able to love and serve God. We are encouraged to help a fellow believer who has stumbled with a firm warning:

> Dear brothers and sisters, if another believer is overcome by some sin, you who are godly should gently and humbly help that person back onto the right path. And be careful not to fall into the same temptation yourself. Share each

other's burdens, and in this way obey the law of Christ. If you think you are too important to help someone, you are only fooling yourself. You are not that important. (Galatians 6:1–3)

But dealing with the addict is no easy task. That's why you must *first* be equipped to understand the *nature* of addiction. Then later you must learn how it can be effectively dealt with. Addiction affects families on varying levels. Family members may not be tempted to *use* the drug but are more likely to fall into the trap of believing the lies of the addict.

To the Non-Believer

Non-believers struggling with addiction have a world of hope awaiting them. They do not yet know or haven't experienced the power of grace and the love of God. However, the battle to find Jesus will be fierce. Just as they were motivated to use a substance to gain a benefit, they will need to feel enough pain from the addiction to seek other options and be open to a spiritual solution.

The 12-step programs work effectively because they are actually spiritual principles. However, the program alone can't replace the need for Jesus Christ Himself. It can, however, help people experience sobriety initially because the principles work. However, people who get sober without Jesus cannot be genuinely transformed. They may be able to stop the insanity of addiction for a season, but long term, they will have a much harder time finding the anchor of their life. Prayerfully, through the twelve steps they could be introduced to Jesus Christ. But if they are not, sobriety alone will not rescue their eternal soul.

Assigning Responsibility

While it's helpful to understand the nature of bondage, doing so doesn't negate the addict's own responsibility. Even as we learn to target Satan as the instigator of addiction, the addict still has a free will (as addressed in Chapter 3). The problem arises when the will is so trapped by the physical, emotional and spiritual aspects of addiction that simply stopping the addiction by choice is very difficult to do. In fact, most often the addict will need to experience more pain than benefit to *adequately* desire change.

Realizing this is important but does not make it an easy truth to grasp. If you are a concerned family member or friend, you have often done everything possible to make the addict stop or to protect the person from hurting himself or herself. But we need to understand that if we prevent addicts from grasping the nature of the problem and from *taking ownership of it*, we can also prevent them from arriving at that place where the addiction is not worth the pain it induces (see Chapter 7).

Understanding the struggle of the addict can help us have more compassion, but at the same time it causes the need for true battle to emerge. The battle against addiction is not directly against the people who are suffering—but against the overall system that has been created in their life. It furthermore can't be waged using human techniques but requires spiritual weapons.

We are human, but we don't wage war as humans do. We use God's mighty weapons, not worldly weapons, to knock down the strongholds of human reasoning and to destroy false arguments. (2 Corinthians 10:3–4)

That's because Satan's strategies, system and devices are beyond our ability to thwart. Gaining the wisdom of God, therefore, is vital. Family members carry their own hurts and guilt in the addiction cycle, but please understand this: Everything God uses to combat addiction will be coated in grace. This means that God isn't here to judge but to deliver the solution. God is the Redeemer, the Rescuer and the Restorer. His truth may offend initially. It may even be painful. But He will bring truth into the life of the addict and the addict's family to release them from Satan's strategies and devices. That's because as Satan is exposed and his system is revealed, everyone involved will have a clear choice to continue to live the lie or to accept and live out the truth. *That simple truth lies at the heart of the beginning of all change.*

"You will know the truth, and the truth will set you free." (John 8:32)

A Prayer for Wisdom

Lord God,

I see this battle that I have been fighting is not against the addict in my life, myself or even an addiction. It's against the enemy. I don't exactly understand how this is possible, but I desire to be equipped to see and know how to handle each situation as it arises. First of all, I make You my Mighty Warrior and my King—I place You above all my own efforts and ask that You secure me with Your weapons of love, grace, truth and forgiveness. Give me eyes to see and perceive the spiritual realm and then fight in the strength of Your might.

In Jesus' name, amen.

CHAPTER 5

A Family Affair

The complexity of the family system that has become aligned with addiction has some distinct characteristics. Whether you are dealing with an actively using addict or one entering into recovery, understanding how addiction has entangled the entire family system is vital. Understanding will also clarify why the addict's recovery process by itself is often not enough to repair overall family problems that have been created.

Family members often feel that the term *recovery* applies only to the person with addiction or other significant problems. However, *true* recovery refers to bringing something back into alignment with its original purpose. For example, when we recover from physical surgery, we are going through a process of healing and being strengthened to return to a certain level of health.

Because the *family system* has typically been so ravaged, it is vital for the family to begin to embrace the fact that they, too, will require a recovery process. In fact, injuries of the heart that occur during the addiction cycle can be more intensive and long lasting than a physical injury. If a broken leg requires a healing process, certainly a deeply wounded heart will require some level of care.

The truth is that addiction has damaged each individual family member in a significant way. As a matter of fact, family members *should hurt*. Being exposed to the horrible realities of addiction is a painful ordeal—and with this, numerous personal violations have usually occurred.

Because family members may experience severe pain and anger in this process, they need to understand the tremendous nature of God's love for the family system as a whole. He wants to restore the fundamental purpose of the family. To do this, He needs to work with *each individual member*. Some family members may require a professional counselor, sponsor or other support system to facilitate healing and help them navigate the recovery process. *Please ask for assistance if you feel overwhelmed at any point.*

To begin this process, we must first see the various levels of breakdown the family has endured in the struggle of addiction. This will be covered in the next two chapters. Looking at areas that are defective or broken is not necessarily pleasant, but it is necessary. From there, we will begin to specify how recovery affects each family member and how God's ultimate goal is to bring restoration when and if possible.

Remember, each situation is unique, and this is only meant to be used as a tool of diagnosis. It is not intended to force anyone to wear a label. Before we move on, let's pray and invite God into your own individual circumstances.

Lord God,

You know what I've been dealing with. You know the pain I have absorbed during _____ addiction. You see what has broken down, and You know that I am weary for peace. God, grant me strength to accept the things that I cannot change, the courage to change the things I can, and the wisdom to know the difference (The Serenity Prayer). In Jesus' name, amen.

God's Purpose for Creating the Family System

God's perfect design for the family system is composed of different roles that can provide for the physical, material, emotional, mental and spiritual needs of each member. These roles are actually designed to reveal different aspects of God's character as a Father, Spouse, Brother and Friend. Each one has a loving and significant purpose. The roles of husband, wife, parent, young children, teens and grown children take on unique tasks and responsibilities. When all member fulfill their parts, these roles are intended to work together much like an orchestra. Each family member is uniquely significant in their "sound," yet when synced with the other members, they create a beautiful "song"—a plan that allows them to fulfill God's purpose on earth by offering a supportive atmosphere for everyone involved.

In this manner, the family system was designed by God to be based on *interdependency*. Members give according to their role and receive according to their legitimate needs. Doing this in the context of God's blueprint for the family will allow family members to be nourished in their basic needs for love, acceptance and security.

While this ideal can be far from reality, it's important that we comprehend God's heart in creating the system itself. (For a full teaching on family systems, we recommend Chapter 2 from *The Christian Codependence Recovery Workbook: From Surviving to Significance.*) His ways are good and right, but living in a broken world often shatters this very precious purpose. Families can be living far from God's plans—attempting instead to survive within a system that is provoking great levels of hurt and pain. The first thing to understand is this painful malfunction wasn't God's intention for the *family* any more than addiction was His plan for the *individual* under its influence.

Satan is the author of sabotaging what God created. What better tactic than to bring a dynamic that offers torment and fear rather than providing safety and love? While seeing this reality is difficult, we must understand that God wants to instigate a process of recovery—if only through the willingness of just one member. This doesn't mean change will happen overnight. Furthermore, it isn't a guarantee that the "perfect" version of a family will spring up in the near future. However, we can move toward His purposes as we become willing to clearly distinguish His plan from a counterfeit version erected in its place, if that applies to our own experience. Furthermore, by using principles of recovery, the family can move toward the original plan (as God authored) through the power of grace.

For this to occur, it's important we begin to grasp the nature of this real war within the family system. We aren't fighting against people, and we most certainly aren't fighting God. In the last chapter, we explored how the addict was captured by Satan's system instead of God's. Exactly *what* the family is coming against should be clear. Families aren't fighting the addict; they are fighting the strategies and devices of the enemy. The Bible highlights this reality.

> For we are not fighting against flesh-and-blood enemies, but against evil rulers and authorities of the unseen world, against mighty powers in this dark world, and against evil spirits in the heavenly places. (Ephesians 6:12)

Our job isn't to fix the system itself but to understand how Satan devises ways to lure people into his operating system. The first way God intervenes is to offer us truth so we begin to shift our focus onto Him. Our willingness to yield to God's perspective will set the course for all necessary change to begin.

The Principle of Homeostasis

God's design for the family in relational dependency revolves around a principle we will refer to in this chapter as *homeostasis*. The dictionary defines *homeostasis* as "the ability or tendency to maintain internal stability in an organism to compensate for environmental changes." Before we get overwhelmed by such a scientific-sounding description, for our purposes we will frame this into a basic concept. On the physical side of life, our bodies have various parts and processes that work together in an interdependent manner. Through the principle of homeostasis, an environment of *regulation* is created that causes the body to maintain a *centering* point that enables stability. From our body temperatures to heartbeats, to blood sugar levels, this internal regulation system dictates a baseline for good health. If any of those levels go too high or too low, the body can become weak, sick or even die. Therefore, when a system is "off" for any reason, the dependent parts will compensate to bring it back in line.

While the healthy function of homeostasis promotes wellness, in some cases the body can be tricked into accepting a *faulty* homeostasis. A person under the influence of substance addiction is one example. The body gets *re*programmed to believe that being under the influence is its healthy point of regulation. It will want to stay under the influence to promote that place of "stability." As a person attempts to purge the chemicals, the body will crave the substance in order to be satisfied and thus return to a place of its *dysfunctional centering*. Imagine the body fighting to maintain the very poison that is killing it!

Homeostasis and the Family System

As we begin to look at the family system through the perspective of homeostasis, we'll find some similarities. The family often tries to maintain a designated point of centering. What drives the centering point will ultimately determine what the family will consider normal. In others words, like the physical body programmed to return a baseline temperature of 98.6 degrees, the family has its own programmed centering. This includes a set of rules, expectations, morals, beliefs and boundaries. The system itself will continually seek to find that ideal balance or regulation. If something or someone brings disruption or change or is simply absent, the other affected members will find a way to bring the system back in line with the centering point.

In a healthy family, the drive to be centered (homeostasis) is formed around God's truth and the guidance of the Holy Spirit. The centering provides not only guidelines but also the resources and power of God to love and to handle life's challenges. The principle of being centered on God means He isn't just a set of rules, but He is an active source of love, availability and authentic interaction. In other words, God the Father, Jesus Christ and the Holy Spirit are *real*—and they are engaged with the family in a relational way.

A Christ-centered family is not perfect. Instead, it has a core reliance on the resources of Jesus Christ. And among them, the power of grace is the resource that handles the problems and deficiencies the family may face. The healthy family will believe that God can meet needs and deal with any challenge or obstacles. It will also rise against anything that would try to take the family away from God.

Addiction in a Christ-Centered Family

In this chapter we will learn how addiction can affect the family's centering point in a negative way. However, it's important to point out first that addiction can manifest in a healthy home. In fact, a family can be centered entirely upon Jesus Christ, and the enemy can find the most vulnerable "victim" to enter through in order to destroy the peace and purpose of that family unit. Remember, Satan's agenda is to destroy what God created as good. It should be no surprise that he would attack a family truly following and serving God.

For example, Jessica took on a rebellious attitude early in high school. Her mom and dad had no idea how to deal with her because they knew in their hearts they had honored the Lord with her life. Her addiction broke their hearts. They were loving, available and authentic Christians. They loved their daughter and taught her healthy boundaries in all facets of relationships and life. To watch her walk away from God and leave them for an addiction was a pain almost unbearable.

In their case, the family system *itself* had a healthy centering. Jessica's parents had strong faith and understood the necessity of God's intervention in her life. Therefore, the addiction was fought against—not welcomed, or accommodated. However, there was a learning process necessary for them to understand how to intervene in a healthy way. Even though Jessica exuded behavior that brought difficult changes to the family system, they could remain focused on the resources of Jesus Christ. They did this by setting boundaries and standing against Jessica's bad behavior.

It's important to highlight that this family was ultimately able to bypass the topics that will be discussed in the next two chapters. Instead, they could go directly to the tools of redemption and intervention (these will be discussed in Chapter 7). Jessica's addiction still hurt them, and they still needed to understand addiction. But they didn't at any level begin to use her addiction as an actual centering point (which most of this chapter will reveal).

If you feel your family fits this scenario, we recommend reading these next two chapters, nonetheless, to gain an understanding of these two realities—a Christ-centered versus an addiction-centered family system. However, you need to apply only that which fits your family's description. Most of us probably fall *somewhere in between the extremes.* However, for teaching purposes, it's helpful to see the more drastic comparisons.

Please also understand that all God's purposes are redemptive. He reveals for one purpose and one purpose alone: *to fix what is broken.*

Addiction-Centered Family System

No matter what behaviors are exemplified, when God's truth and His Spirit are not influencing the center of a family system, a human system is devised. This means the homeostasis (centering point) is someone or something other than God. The actual person that becomes the centering role within a family system may vary and can at times fluctuate. **This may or may not be the person with the actual addiction.** It is crucial to understand that whatever is influencing the controlling person(s) will determine what occurs.

Often addiction and the addict become the family system's centering point. Everyone in the family other than the addict is using the addiction-driven influence to direct how they should respond. For example, Jack was the leader and controlling influence of his family. This would be perfectly healthy if he were operating by God-dependency. But Jack was an alcoholic and emotionally broken and had extreme mood swings that led to violent behavior. On his good days, everyone was allowed to be happy. But when Jack was in a "bad mood," everyone knew and had to accommodate accordingly. The homeostasis of that family rested on *Jack's* needs. Everyone else was meant to work around that basic central purpose. Because his leadership style was so unhealthy, it turned the family into a prison rather than a free environment.

In every family system, the person who assumes the central role sets the tone for the beliefs, standards, rules and boundaries that will be implemented in the home. Usually, this system develops through *unspoken* messages and rules that are simply imposed and indirectly expected. Examples of this may include statements like these: "We don't talk about our feelings" or "We work hard to make sure Dad isn't angry." Unlike the healthy family that can use God's Word as a handbook to understand God's perspective, the unhealthy family system is operating from no direct source except the person running it. Since that person's mood, emotions and spiritual influences may fluctuate, the family's point of reference is also asked to conform to the need. This is one reason there is such insecurity in an unhealthy family system—no one can predict or understand what to expect in any given moment.

Learning what or who centers a home will shed light on the overall system, but it isn't meant to turn into a battle against that person alone. Rather, it's meant to expose and clearly distinguish God's plans from a system that contradicts them. In this next section, we will examine how to compare and contrast the characteristics of a family system led by a Christ-centered homeostasis versus one driven by an unhealthy human agenda.

Love versus Selfishness

God's love is not a feeling—it's a power source that leads to action. However, His love *is* affectionately interested in our well-being. He will promote any agenda that will align us with our God-given purpose and identity. If our Heavenly Father must confront, correct, discipline or expose uncomfortable truths, it's because He hates and is jealous of the things that harm us. It is *never* to harm us with malicious intent.

God's love doesn't guarantee that we will be happy, however. Not only do we live in a broken world that brings suffering, but God is most motivated by our deeper spiritual needs. That means when we want Him to fix something, He may allow us—in different seasons—to experience pain and suffering *instead.* Through these trials and tribulations, the Word of God promises that God can reveal Himself to us. God wants us to learn how to walk in the power of His love rather than under the challenge of our circumstances. *That doesn't dismiss or minimize authentic pain.* In fact, God's love promotes our ability to express our pain and feel grief (Romans 8:26). However, God's love interacts with us at our *true need* to teach us to trust Him, rely on Him and receive what we need from Him. From there, He even promises to use ALL things together for our good (Romans 8:28). He knows that a life apart from Him leads to destruction, but a life in Him leads to fullness and peace. Therefore, He seeks to eradicate the things in our lives that make us "sick" so we can maintain a vibrant, healthy centering point on Him. When we are aligned and living under God's homeostatic environment, we are free to become all He created us to be. *True love will promote this at all costs.*

The love of God is one of the most confusing areas in the Christian life because we often misunderstand both its source and its agenda. First, God's love is not a human resource. Rather, His love comes through a connection to Him. The Holy Spirit injects love into us, and then we have the capability to give it away to others. That doesn't mean we can't have a *form* of love, but human love will always fall short and doesn't have the power to overcome the effects of sin's harm.

In the design of the family, God developed all roles with the intent that His love would be driving and influencing their purposes. It was never meant that one person do all the loving and another all the receiving. In fact, a family cannot remain healthy unless everyone is carrying their own supply. Through love, all rules, agendas and overall interactions will promote the well-being of each member. Thus, it will create an environment that will not care about happiness in the moment but instead will care about spiritual and emotional needs with more long-term ramifications.

One of the most significant breakdowns in the family system occurs when love isn't the driving force. When love is not present, a selfish system typically takes its place. This creates a dynamic in which a *person* begins to satisfy a *personal* agenda that will promote their *own* needs and interests. The cost of having those needs met may harm others. People become mere instruments of fulfilling those personal interests. As horrible as it sounds, most family members of an addict understand this firsthand. They have witnessed an addict's behavior revolve around this very dynamic.

A family system that operates by trying to satisfy the priority of one *person* rather than a system centered on *God* has more ramifications than we can mention in this brief chapter. It is the awful reality of life apart from God. We can be deceived and operate this way without even knowing it. However, God's love doesn't beat us over the head by exposing inappropriately centered areas. Rather, His love offers us an *understanding* of what we've accepted as "normal" centering but is far from His intent.

Freedom versus Control

We will learn repeatedly in this book that the essence of God's love to us is expressed through free will. God gave us the incredible gift of choice that allows us to decide how to interact with Him and others. Had God not offered us this relational style, we'd be enslaved to Him by force. We'd be like preprogrammed machines used to perform a function rather than engage intimately and through love. Therefore, while God desires that we give Him control, He makes it optional. He is a Leader who respects His followers and doesn't "cram" Himself down their throats.

When God isn't in control, a human system takes His place of authority. In fact, when we aren't allowing God to be in control, it often means we are in the operating seat. Or we may have allowed someone or something else to make decisions on our behalf. Human-controlled structures will always bring damage. That's because human beings could never offer the resources God Almighty provides! Even the most well-intentioned human lacks the wisdom, pure love and power to act on our behalf. Imagine comparing the strength of a gnat with that of a lion—there *is* no comparison! Comparing human strength with God's power is insanely ridiculous. God is the Potter; we are the clay. The clay can't independently grow in beauty and design unless it is allowed to be shaped by the Maker.

In dealing with the dynamic of control, we must discover what we have allowed to influence us and how that has shaped our own lives. We are going to highlight two forms of control: Aggressive and Passive.

1. Aggressive control.

Some families operate under a "dictatorship" form of control. In this system, family members are told how to think, feel and make choices. They do not enjoy individual rights, nor are they allowed to do anything apart from the leadership's approval. As members begin to serve this unhealthy system, their own unique needs, feelings and personal identities are diminished. Thus, in order to survive, they resort to role-playing, where they learn to hide their authentic selves (these roles will be discussed in Chapter 6). The members learn to submit in order to please and accommodate the person(s) in the controlling role rather than to give love.

When one member controls aggressively, the other members form a system of counter-control. They may also opt to rebel against the system altogether.

While it may sound incredibly "evil" and be something that would not happen in a Christian family, this is simply not true. A Christian who hasn't processed through their own emotional issues or is under the influence of a substance can take on these characteristics.

The person operating by an aggressive form of control may be abusive, raging and bent on a strategy of self-gain. It must be recognized that this is a *spiritual* condition. That doesn't make it okay. It will be necessary to deal with an ultra-controlling dynamic.

2. Passive control.

A control-based system can happen through "good" efforts to help, fix and solve the problems of other members. In this system, there isn't direct dictatorship, but rather the loss of choices and the merging of identities (defined as *codependence* in a later chapter). In passive control, a person's problems and needs become "community property." Instead of that person owning their own problems, the passive-controlling family members take ownership for them. In this system, the person in control is often *trying* to "love," but instead is imposing his or her own will on the other members.

For example, Paula loved her daughter April and had been extremely involved in all aspects of her life. But from a young age and through early adulthood, April wasn't given permission to make her own decisions. No matter what she did, her mom voiced an opinion and disallowed April's own thoughts and choices to mandate her decisions. When April made a bad choice that opposed her mom's suggestion, she was given shame-based statements that told her she was only successful when she took her mother's advice.

While Paula genuinely thought she was helping, she created a controlling dynamic. She also attached herself to her daughter in an unhealthy manner by doing things *for* her that April should have done on her own. April wasn't allowed to be an adult, to take ownership of her free will or to make decisions and reap the benefits or consequences. She eventually opted to seize a lifestyle of rebellion and drug use. That didn't make it her mother's *fault*, but since April felt unable to please or leave her mother's grip, she eventually left altogether.

While good intentions usually drive the passive-controller, we must understand that humans weren't designed to have another human operating their wills. Thus, when that occurs, there will be a toxic reaction to it. Anyone exerting this type of control is misunderstanding authentic love. It is a condition of the soul that must be recentered and realigned to Holy Spirit love.

It's imperative that we understand the general dynamics of a human-controlled system versus a Holy Spirit-controlled environment. That's because all forms of family breakdowns will result from that nature of control. As we have already learned, when the family is under human control, the homeostasis of that family will be sick rather than healthy.

Nothing is permanent. God can change the dynamics of unhealthy control. However, the power of change will happen as individual wills come under the influence of God's will. If you suffer from either form of control, it's not something you can change overnight. However, it is something that recovery will walk you through. In fact, it is where all change begins.

Meditation Points:

Do you recognize control in your own family system? How do you feel controlled? Do you attempt to control others?

_____

_____

_____

_____

Truth versus Lies

Truth is God's method of leading us into paths instigated by His wisdom and understanding. Truth is not subject to personal interpretation as much of our culture suggests. It is concretely founded on the character of God and revealed in the Word of God. Truth acts like a flashlight to illuminate the direction and purposes God has in each situation. Thus, when we walk outside of truth, we are walking in darkness. Because we cannot see which steps to take, we can be overcome by all sorts of dangerous realities. It should be obvious that truth is a powerful and potent force!

In the unhealthy, addiction-centered family system, not only is truth absent, but there is also often an unspoken rule that no one speaks the truth. Usually, a form of denial is covering the family and prevents the members from seeing the reality of what is occurring (biblically known as *walking in darkness*). For example, David often heard, "Davy, Daddy has a stomach ache and needs to stay home. Make your daddy some soup." In truth, his dad was an alcoholic and would be passed out to the point of incoherence. For David to function in this system, he was asked to be part of the lie. No one could admit or speak of the addiction openly; rather they compensated, adjusted and lived under the power of that lie. This obstructed David's ability to see truth in his life in general. He thought it was normal to make up stories, lie and deny. David also found it a "normal" relationship skill to accommodate wrong behavior rather than recognize or confront it.

To operate under a lie may sound evil or bad, but it is really more a matter of being *deceived.* Family members end up serving a lie by doing what they believe will please or help the struggling member. Children are especially prone to this, making it that much more heartbreaking in its innocent intent. We can't downplay the effects of a lie. All lies need to be uprooted and replaced with truth. They will disrupt, harm and cause deep pain to those who come under their effects. That's why everyone involved in the addiction cycle will benefit from seeking the truth.

Meditation Point:
While it can be difficult to assess, do you see lies and denial in your family? Describe one example.

Grace versus Shame

God provided us with the most amazing human remedy imaginable—a resource that could continually deal with weaknesses, difficulties, needs, mistakes, sinful choices and violations. This resource contains His ability to make up for what we can't accomplish on our own. It's called *grace*. Grace is what takes us into relationship with God initially and also gives us the ability to have an ongoing connection to Him. Grace sees life through lenses of what God can do for us rather than the lenses of what we are doing wrong.

Addiction-centered families are dealing with a constant onslaught of problems, sin issues, violations and other painful realities. Because there is so much "wrong" at so many levels, if grace isn't present, shame will by default become the operating system. That's because shame is the direct residue of sin. It promotes an overall sense of defectiveness. When we feel shame, we feel a pervasive sense that we don't measure up. Shame speaks messages to the family that say, "Something is wrong with us and we need to hide." The very nature of shame is to cover. Thus, in the case of addiction, there is an unspoken rule that no one talks or allows others to know what's really going on. This leads to isolation.

A shame-based family can also be prone to being behaviorally and image-oriented. As long as it "looks" good—then it *is* good (so it seems). It can promote performance over authentic needs. Therefore, instead of talking about problems, fears and pain, those feelings can be repressed with the emphasis placed on outward behavior.

For example, Joseph was a pastor and thus held an image in his church and community. But because he hadn't dealt with his own emotional brokenness, he formed a shame-based system in the family system as a whole. It didn't mean Joseph didn't genuinely love and want to serve God. But his own fear of rejection and need for image maintenance surpassed his ability to admit his struggles to anyone. Therefore, instead of being able to work through his issues, he hid and suppressed them. Over time, the pressure of the ministry caused Joseph to be more and more consumed by emotional brokenness. Joseph had fits of rage in his family, all the while maintaining an outward image of love to the church community. The family learned to compensate and adjust around Joseph's issues and learned how to play the charade of "everything is fine" when in fact it wasn't. In fact, Joseph's emotional problems began to dictate the *center* of the family. As shame permeated the system, everyone felt there was something wrong.

When a son began using drugs, the family responded to addiction as it responded to Joseph's own emotional challenges—they denied the truth of what was happening. Hiding, pretending, and using rage to try to bring the son "in line" led to a family that was fundamentally broken, causing members to hide, to fear and to be unable to articulate their honest thoughts, feeling and needs.

It must be understood that shame is a tool of the enemy, not of God. Shame has no real leverage in the life of a believer. God has eradicated shame through the cross. However, shame can be given allowance in our lives when we measure ourselves by anything else *but* the cross. That's because we are incapable of being good enough on our own. But through grace, we are given an unconditional seal of approval. For both the addict and family members, authentic Christian recovery is about ridding ourselves of all forms of shame. If you recognize its presence, be assured it's one of the areas God wants to work through. That's why a Christ-centered recovery approach isn't just a *little* different—it holds the potent key to true and long-lasting solutions.

Meditation Point:
Describe how shame affects your family.

_____
_____
_____
_____

Pleasing God versus Pleasing People

A family centered on the Lord will accept what will promote its well-being and reject that which will cause harm. As much as family members love one another, they will recognize that only in following God's truth can anyone truly receive proper help.

When addiction-centered mentalities prevail, loyalty doesn't promote the safety, security and love meant to bind the members together. Instead, loyalty ends up protecting the very things that are hurting the family. This loyalty may be "never call the cops" after a family member is badly beaten. It can say "never talk to anyone about my family problems" to the teenage girl whose world is falling apart. Or it can pronounce "stand by my husband when he asks me to call him in sick."

Because the family is centered on the person they are serving rather than on God's truth, bad behaviors and lies become an acceptable method of functioning. For example, young Betty's mom was an alcoholic and this became "normal" to Betty. So did Betty's assuming the mom role for her four-year-old sister. Betty's world was filled with a faulty system that dictated how she should respond. But Betty learned from an early age to be loyal to her mom and the family code of never talking about what was wrong. She served the "center" place of mom's needs, and her role was to adapt and compensate for anything that was missing. Utter loyalty was rooted deeply, and Betty would defend and protect her mother at any expense, even as a grown adult.

Loyalty is a noble character trait. Family members are deceived into thinking their loyalty is a powerful form of expressing love. However, loyalty to a toxic system will bring significant damage. There is only one cure: To first filter everything through "is it pleasing to God?" God has a remedy for the problems and a strategy and cure for those who are struggling. Our loyalty to Him can therefore be translated into loyalty for others. *We can learn to help people as God would help them.*

Meditation Point:
Have you ever been loyal to the addict, even when their behavior was wrongful or unhealthy?

_____
_____
_____
_____
_____

Healthy Intimacy and Identity versus Faulty Role-Playing

Intimacy is the ability to see into someone and let them see into you. It validates and affirms the personal identity of someone. God created us to relate first to Him intimately and be vulnerable and real with Him. He created the family system to mimic this same intimacy. In fact, the family is meant to be a safe haven where we can come as we are and find acceptance and love. It won't encourage our wrongful behaviors, but it will continue to love us through our areas of weakness.

When the family system breaks down, intimacy is impossible. We cannot reveal our needs or weaknesses in an environment where they will be used against us. Thus, in the unhealthy family system, members end up covering their authentic selves by an outward role. (We will discuss this in detail in Chapter 6.) Instead of sharing authentic thoughts, feelings and needs, families who lack intimacy end up developing their own coping mechanisms and live their inner lives apart from their outer lives.

When these dynamics are in place, family members won't only experience the pain of that system, but they also risk losing themselves altogether. This has the potential for enormous consequences.

God's heart operates by intimacy. Even when intimacy is not immediately attainable in the family system, it will be accessible from Him immediately. His priority for individuals is to develop a healthy identity so they can see who they are from *His* perspective.

Meditation Point:

Does your family have intimacy problems? Can people share and love from the heart, or is there distance, isolation and avoidance?

_____

_____

_____

_____

_____

Real versus Counterfeit

We've spent time developing an idea of the character and heart of God as it relates to the family system. It should be obvious that, even as Christians, we aren't necessarily operating by these principles. Perhaps no one will ever fully live and function by healthy principles all the time. However, it's God's desire that we learn how to align to Him in detailed ways.

A family can operate many ways apart from the Spirit of God. Sometimes, God is blatantly disrespected and unwelcome in a household. Thus, His presence and influence aren't allowed. But in Christian families, God can be discussed to a degree but used in a way that is shaming and rule oriented. When spirituality is displayed by invoking God's name to inflict guilt, shame, control or fear, it is not coming from the Holy Spirit. That's because the Holy Spirit operates through love, grace, peace and holiness. False spirituality is just as toxic as no spirituality at all. It creates a version that can totally oppose the heart and character of God.

It should be understood that this is a symptom of a deeper spiritual problem. Many people don't walk with God in love and authentic empowerment—not because they don't want to—but because they don't know who He is. Religious mentalities seek to create God as someone oriented toward performance and checklists. Agnostics deny His power and deity altogether. In either case, misconceptions could be swallowed up in a moment if that person had a personal encounter with the living God of the universe!

Overcoming a misunderstanding of God is a personal journey for each family member. Even if one member gains a rightful perspective of Him, it cannot be imposed onto the other members. However, anyone who houses His authentic love will have the option of representing Him in a true way. Sometimes entire families are brought into reconciliation in this manner—one person at a time.

Meditation Point*:*

What is your own perspective of God? How has He been represented in your own family experience past and present?

_____

_____

_____

_____

_____

What to Do

When a faulty centering has been created in the system, its roots and symptoms can run deep. Your response to this material may be a sense of pain, anger, confusion or curiosity. Be assured, the only intent in reviewing these concepts is to prepare for healthy interaction. Our prayer is that if the addict in your life gets well, you too can prepare to live out a healthy homeostasis. Prayerfully, this can be a *together*-journey! But for now, it's best that the addict and the family work through these issues individually. For now, everyone involved needs an understanding.

Your assurance of this process is that God is interested in you, not just your interaction with the addict, *but you.* Thus, He will personally meet you wherever you may be.

In the next chapter, we will look at how the individual roles break down and produce something we'll refer to as a *survival system.* But for now, take some time to invite God into your own situation.

A Prayer for My Family

Lord Jesus,

I pray over the center of my family. I pray that we would submit ourselves to You at an authoritative level. If I'm in that position, please grant me the strength and ability to give that position to You. If I'm in a supportive role, help me be true to You despite the other system at play. Teach me how to do this.

In Jesus' name, amen.

CHAPTER 6

Surviving the Storm

Most of us are familiar with the television show *Survivor*. It is a reality game show that tests contestants' ability to withstand the brutal, threatening environments of the raw outdoors. People are forced to deal with nature without modern-day resources and technology. The purpose is to discover who is strong enough to survive the elements of weather, terrain and all sorts of dangerous circumstances.

The popularity of the show reveals how "surviving" is applauded by society. It can seem that the goal of survival is to be the greatest and the strongest. But in God's world, mere survival is never a goal. That's because He didn't create the human race to find ways to survive. He created us for relationship, intimacy and connection. Relationship with Him is based on security of the highest magnitude; thus, no one who claims to be His son or daughter has the need to "survive." But it goes even further. We need not survive without resources because we have everything we need in and through Him (Philippians 4:19). While this promise is wonderful and alluring, getting it from the head to the heart is a journey.

God is never interested in finger-pointing for the purpose of faultfinding. Instead, He is passionately interested in *helping* us attain all the resources we need to be free in Him. As He injects His own abilities into our life circumstances, we begin to have tools to deal with the challenges.

Survival roles in the family system are a difficult dynamic because they run deep— even to the point of becoming a person's *identity*. And while they *do* defend us from some level of harm, they prevent us from living within our true potential and identity in Christ. Thus understanding these principles is a critical part of every family member's recovery process.

In this chapter we will break down the survival roles that are developed to deal with an unhealthy control-based system as diagnosed in Chapter 5. While each system is entirely different, we can draw some similarities.

Addiction and Survival

As we learned in the last chapter, when the homeostasis of a family is unhealthy, the centering place or "normal" state can actually be destructive or toxic. To make better sense of this reality, we might visualize the site of a catastrophic tornado that tore through a neighborhood. Debris, rubbish and destruction would be strewn in the very places meant to house a community. As a result, the foundational purpose of that neighborhood would be destroyed. A rebuilding process would be necessary to realign it to its intended purpose.

Now, imagine that families remained in the storm site. Instead of cleaning and rebuilding, they tried to survive off the remnants of their destroyed possessions because they didn't want to face the devastation of the loss. For them, living with the *familiar* provided a comfort; thus, they had no interest in rebuilding.

It may seem insane, but in many ways the family system operating with an addictive-based center does just that. Instead of a centering place ordained by God to represent connection and safety, a disaster site is maintained. And where a safe haven was meant to provide security, survival in "raw" conditions requires adaptive skills. Anyone living in this manner will take on a *survival mind-set* in which the lack of necessities must be overcome by alternative strategies.

When Survival Turns Dangerous

Survival mode has an instinctual purpose. God gave our physical bodies survival instincts to deal with major traumatic events. However, survival is not meant to become a way of life. FEMA (Federal Emergency Management Agency) provided temporary housing to people following the horrible storm Katrina. These homes allowed families to survive when their own homes had been destroyed. In the midst of the crisis, a temporary home was a better alternative than living in the street. Yet these homes were meant to be used strictly through the crisis; they weren't intended to be a long-term lifestyle. However, tragically, some families couldn't afford to purchase another home and lived in these temporary shelters for several years. Over time the very homes meant to sustain in an imminent crisis apparently became toxic. Reports indicate the occupants of this housing complained a few years later of breathing difficulties, nosebleeds and persistent headaches. United States health officials admitted that tests found potentially hazardous levels of toxic formaldehyde gas had formed. What is the lesson? The homes had a purpose, but long-term use was never intended. And when they were used in that manner, an entire new level of problems was created.

In the same manner, when trauma or unhealthy centering harms a family, some survival skills may be required simply to get through the situation. But when this modified system becomes the long-term lifestyle, everyone will get sick. Compensation roles are essentially like FEMA homes being used in the midst of the rubbish. The reason they are used may be perfectly legitimate and needful. However, the long-term remedy and the power to rebuild the beautiful home that was lost can only happen through the hands and heart of the Creator of the universe. It isn't a human process at all; it's a process that requires divine power.

Family members have often learned how to survive in various unhealthy ways. Most people who have adapted unhealthy coping mechanisms don't even recognize them as such because they have become accustomed to them. The first way to evaluate whether unhealthy compensation (survival) roles exist is to determine whether their fruits exist. Like the physical symptoms that occurred because of overused FEMA housing, we can recognize toxic residue within by the manifestation of symptoms. When it's present, we experience shame, guilt, fear, loss of identity, anxiety, panic, anger, burnout, control and the hardening of the emotional life. Furthermore, we are problem-oriented and chronically aware of the unmet needs.

Adaptive/Survival Roles in the Addiction-Based Family System

In understanding your own storm site, you too must see if or how you've entered a survival role. At first this can be difficult to recognize because these roles often complement aspects of our authentic personalities. The purpose of this next section is merely to *identify*, not to point, blame or label. By assigning each family member (or close relationship) a survival role, we can begin to identify the patterns of balance, control and unhealthy coping. We can see the cause and effect one family member's role has on all the others (the principle of homeostasis). To visualize this, refer to *The Addiction-Based Family System* on page 56. Imagine this diagram being an actual mobile with hanging parts that work together to produce a centering. The linked family roles have methods of compensation or survival that affect the system as a whole. We are going to take a closer look at each role.

Behavioral/Chemically Addicted Personality

Behaviorally/Chemically Addictive Personalities (BCAPs) usually take the position of centering; thus, all other roles adapt around and seek to align with their needs. These personalities can be dominating, angry and controlling yet charming, sensitive and kind. BCAPs typically have manipulative personalities that will accommodate whatever is needed to keep them in control. They have often gained a sense of entitlement within their family systems and feel perfectly justified in having other members serve their needs. BCAPs have broken issues at their cores but have learned to attach to a substance or other coping mechanism to deal with them. They are not able to love or be intimate in a healthy way.

While it can appear that these roles are always wrapped around active addiction, there are frequent exceptions. In fact, there may be another person in the family dealing with substance addiction while BCAPs simply have an unhealthy relationship style of control and domination.

If BCAPs do have chemical addictions and at some point "sober up" without authentic recovery, their personalities will not change. They can sometimes be even more challenging to deal with since they are typically very unhappy, depressed, angry and detached. That's because the lifestyle of BCAPs revolve around acting out of deeply rooted issues. BCAPs need help, but their systems of control and domination will need to be confronted. This can be a very difficult task. If or when these personalities do enter recovery, an unusual change will occur. Since BCAPs were controlling figures of their homes, the change will cause a deep disturbance in the family system's balance structure. This could lead to a positive change if brought under a centering in Christ.

While BCAPs can be difficult, these people are in need of intervention and love. BCAPs' greatest need will be to process emotional pain and effectively heal through the process of

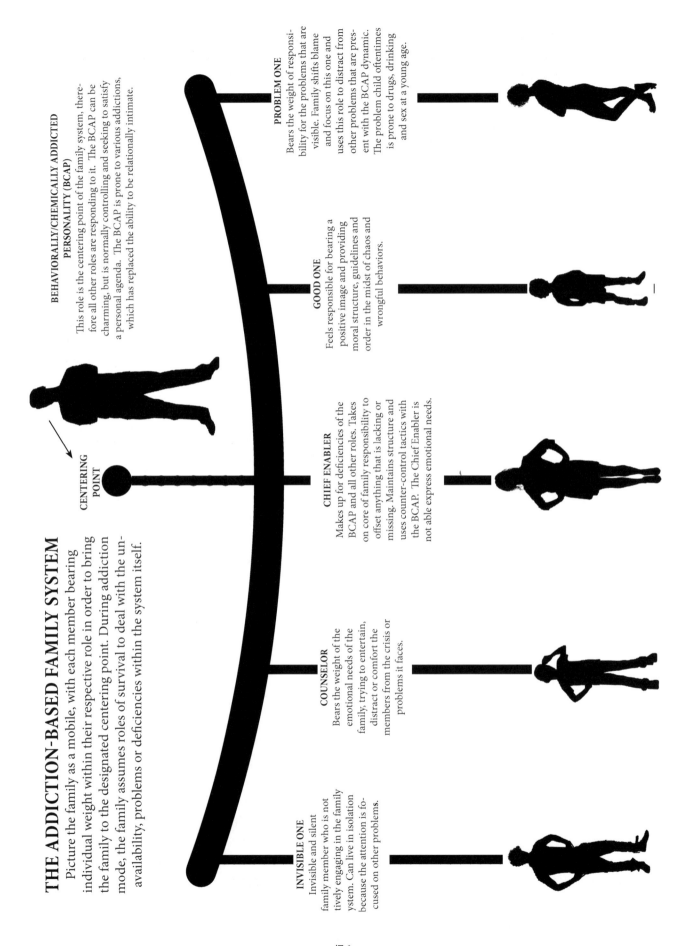

THE ADDICTION-BASED FAMILY SYSTEM

Picture the family as a mobile, with each member bearing individual weight within their respective role in order to bring the family to the designated centering point. During addiction mode, the family assumes roles of survival to deal with the unavailability, problems or deficiencies within the system itself.

CENTERING POINT

BEHAVIORALLY/CHEMICALLY ADDICTED PERSONALITY (BCAP)

This role is the centering point of the family system, therefore all other roles are responding to it. The BCAP can be charming, but is normally controlling and seeking to satisfy a personal agenda. The BCAP is prone to various addictions, which has replaced the ability to be relationally intimate.

PROBLEM ONE

Bears the weight of responsibility for the problems that are visible. Family shifts blame and focus on this one and uses this role to distract from other problems that are present with the BCAP dynamic. The problem child oftentimes is prone to drugs, drinking and sex at a young age.

GOOD ONE

Feels responsible for bearing a positive image and providing moral structure, guidelines and order in the midst of chaos and wrongful behaviors.

CHIEF ENABLER

Makes up for deficiencies of the BCAP and all other roles. Takes on core of family responsibility to offset anything that is lacking or missing. Maintains structure and uses counter-control tactics with the BCAP. The Chief Enabler is not able express emotional needs.

COUNSELOR

Bears the weight of the emotional needs of the family, trying to entertain, distract or comfort the members from the crisis or problems it faces.

INVISIBLE ONE

Invisible and silent family member who is not actively engaging in the family system. Can live in isolation because the attention is focused on other problems.

recovery. Sobriety, along with a Christ-centered approach to life and relationships, will be imperative (if applicable) for healing to occur. Learning the love of God is the beginning of all freedom for BCAPs.

"Chief Enablers"

Where there is an addict, typically enablers have also sprung up to deal with the needs and deficiencies of the "storm site." These personalities are typically very controlling and ultra-responsible out of what is perceived as necessity. Chief Enablers learn to adapt around people who are unavailable. Thus, wherever needs exist, Chief Enablers "fill in the gap." Chief Enablers usually carry the driving force behind their families to "keep things afloat." They can work three jobs, run a household and participate in ministry all at the same time. However, they are usually extremely out of touch with emotions and thus live in deep denial. Their external lives often do not connect with their inner lives. They may be bitter, angry and resentful. Yet they may, at the same time, be sweet and accommodating.

Chief Enablers are in desperate need of recovery in order to understand their seemingly "good" deeds are in fact a danger to themselves and others. The imbalanced mentality of Chief Enablers usually seeps into all aspects of life; thus, compensating becomes a lifestyle. Therefore, Chief Enablers will carry an unhealthy perspective of relationships in all facets of their lives. This is also known as *codependency*. They believe they are meant to do the giving but usually get nothing or little in return.

Through recovery, Chief Enablers will learn to assert boundaries and stop taking ownership of other people's problems. Their greatest need is to get in touch with their own feelings, attitudes, beliefs, thoughts and motivations. Most important, they will need to reclaim their authentic identities. In essence, they will need to have their wills detached from a people-centered influence to a God-centered position.

It's important to note these personalities are prone to becoming chemically addicted and at some point even leave these roles and take on the characteristics of BCAPs.

Chief Enablers will experience enormous relief through the recovery process. But learning how to release management of all the family's needs and problems will take time. Chief Enablers in recovery need time, space and grace to learn how to untangle themselves from a role that has, at times, promoted the addiction cycle. They will benefit from learning about a loving, connected and intimate God who is motivated by love.

When Chief Enablers receive recovery *first*, it will disrupt the balance of the family system and create a gaping hole in its ability to function. With God's help, this can be positive and establish the potential for a new system based on grace to resurrect in the place of the old system. However, this may not happen overnight, and the process itself can be messy. Therefore, it's essential that Chief Enablers in recovery have strong supportive bases.

"Good Ones"

In a dysfunctional family system, a common adaption entails an ultra-responsible role. Good Ones usually go to great measures to do everything right, please everyone and make their families "look good." While Chief Enablers manage everything, Good Ones are very rule oriented and legalistic. They live their lives with a measuring stick. While they may be achieving this role at an external level, Good Ones never feel validated or good enough. Shame begins to coat Good Ones' identities, driving them to try harder.

People in this role are usually prone to find unhealthy relationships that perpetuate their own positions of "being good." They unknowingly attract people who are "less than" in order to stay elevated in their positions.

This personality needs recovery from *codependency* in order to break free from these destructive patterns. That's because their entire lifestyle is usually formed around shame. If left without recovery, Good Ones can continue down the pathway of performance, perfectionism and status. However, it should be noted that Good Ones may sometimes check out with substance use after becoming exhausted with failed efforts. Thus, they end up doing the exact opposite of what this role originally entailed.

Good Ones will be completely transformed through a recovery process that introduces God's love and grace. Although there are prideful tendencies, they are usually rooted in deeper levels of pain and a sense of never being enough. Through recovery, this can be swallowed by God's love. When Good Ones are in recovery, the other family members will be perplexed. It can be confusing when the one who seemed to have it together is admitting problems. This may bring relief to the other members or give them the opportunity to deal with their own problems. Or it might scare or offend the others who are witnessing the Good One's changes.

"Family Counselors"

Often a family member can sense the deep pain in the family system and feel obligated to change it. Family Counselors work in various ways to try to fix what's wrong. Unlike the other roles, Family Counselors are especially in tune with emotional needs. Thus, this compensation role may try to make the family happy by always joking and finding comic relief to distract the family. Or they may resort to a more serious role of supporting the emotional needs of each member. A *child* in this role may actually be the one the parents rely on to discuss problems. But because this role places the weight of the problems onto that member (especially a child) in an unhealthy way, many negative symptoms will result. Family Counselors feel responsible for the needs and problems of others and will incorporate this as a normal interaction in all their relationship**s**.

Family Counselors usually go into the service industry—or enter a professional role of caregiving. While always focusing on the needs of others, they are unable to take care of *self*. This can lead to physical, emotional and spiritual problems of every magnitude.

In recovery, Family Counselors must learn self-care. They need to learn that authentic love must first be received before it can be given. They will need to practice a season of focusing on their own needs more than trying to resolve other people's problems.

When Family Counselors enter recovery and become less available, it can be painful for others. There can be a sense of letdown and rejection when Family Counselors don't fulfill needs. However, when the Family Counselors step aside, other members have a better chance of learning to go directly to God to get their needs met. Family Counselors must learn throughout recovery to make this the goal of each relationship, yet learn to love and support the members in a healthy and honoring way.

"Invisible Ones"

This role hides from the family system through outward activities or diversions. By being unavailable and swept away in a fantasyland, Invisible Ones don't have to feel or deal with reality. While Invisible Ones don't cause many problems, they are often like a bomb waiting to explode. Their lack of relational skills leaves this role very vulnerable to extremely unhealthy behavior. This may include pornography, addiction, violence and even unexpected rage. Invisible Ones are more prone to suicide than the other personalities.

In the family's homeostasis, Invisible Ones don't offer much to their families one way or another. Thus, this role is somewhat neutral. Although quiet, it is unpredictable and is prone to create chaos at any given point.

Invisible Ones can sometimes be the most difficult to access. Their realities may be built around the world of electronic media. The resulting lack of intimacy and relational skills make it even harder to communicate and understand their authentic needs. They desperately need help but oftentimes will refuse it.

In recovery, Invisible Ones must learn to *feel emotions*. They will come in touch with an active, caring and relational God. *He* will need to do the work of thawing the heart. In fact, the injection of intimacy is perhaps the greatest need of all. Only the Holy Spirit can do this deeper work. It will be a process and require a social setting such as a meeting in order to help steer away from the mind-set of isolation.

When the Invisible One recovers, the other family members will see a tremendous change. It may not prompt any dramatic shifts in the family balance, but it will prompt curiosity and interest in what is happening in his or her life.

"Problem Ones"

Problem Ones opt not to follow the family system, resorting to rebellious behaviors and attitudes. Therefore, it's easy for the other members to blame Problem Ones for family trouble. Usually (though not always) they are just acting out the dysfunction their families already contain. The basic mind-set of Problem Ones is to resist authority and create their own rules. Thus, they often struggle in school and get in trouble with the law. The Problem Ones are almost always engaged in a chemical lifestyle and are usually involved in unhealthy sexual relationships. While they leave the family system, they often attach to friends in a family manner. The loyalty of friends becomes extreme and in many ways replaces the function intended for the family of origin. Problem Ones can absorb their families' attention or can compete with the primary addict's position. Children in this position can often become their families' center with the potential to become future BCAPs. If there is another addict in the home, the two separate addict mind-sets can create even more chaos as each one tries to absorb the center role.

Problem Ones are *acting out,* and while seeming "bad," they actually have inner wounds screaming to be addressed. It's not uncommon for them to be very sensitive and caring despite their wrongful behavior. Problem Ones learn extremely unhealthy ways to deal with pain. Often that pain is legitimate, but their methods of coping and survival create toxic patterns. They will have unlimited and unthinkable pain and suffering without intervention—and are prone to patterns of addiction throughout their lifetime.

In recovery, Problem Ones will benefit from the power of forgiveness, redemption and

Christ-centered identity. They will be able to reflect a profound and tangible representation of God's healing capability. However, their process may take time. Their wounds usually go deeper, and their changes may also be slower.

Other family members will pay attention to the Problem Ones' changes. It may cause discomfort in these family systems because the Problem Ones can no longer be blamed. In some families, some members will actually want to continue to label the Problem Ones as having problems even after recovery. This makes the Problem Ones' individual recovery extremely important.

Separating a Person from Behavior

One of the more difficult tasks for family members to learn is how to separate an *addict*, or other family roles, from his or her actual *behavior* (refer to Chapter 1). The fruit in an addict's life can and should be hated. But the addict is under the influence and needs to be loosed from the addiction's grip. But this isn't only true for the BCAP; it's also true for all the other roles. The adaptive roles have an influence. Therefore, even when they produce seemingly "good" behavior, they can in fact be toxic underneath.

To clarify further, imagine each *role* we learned about as an actual *costume* that is worn in order to function in the home. Costumes provide a covering to create a separate reality for the purpose of performance. For example, Disneyland has many different characters come to life through people in costumes. As well as these characters perform their roles, those costumes are removed at the end of the day, and the actors return to their authentic selves. Although some of their natural characteristics may complement the role, who they are and the roles they play are entirely different.

Addiction (and all adaptive roles) are similar—but they aren't quite as simple as costumes you can put on and take off instantly. Everyone ends up wearing a "costume" that projects a reality different from their authentic identity. Eventually, this becomes normal and an environment is produced where only "costumes" are acceptable. Thus, family members can't escape wearing and functioning in them.

Rescuing us from Costumes

God created us for freedom and wholeness. He knows who we really are because He created us for purpose and significance in His image. When we live apart from Him by focusing on an alternative centering point, He sees us in these dreadful costumes that were never authorized by Him. Knowing us as His beautiful and precious children, He longs to return us to His original design. God's love is tender, but it is willing to break down those toxic costumes. To do this, He works with us using intentional and loving methods. But as we will learn, God's love is tough and will use the weapon of pain to break through those faulty survival roles and rescue us individually.

From here on out, we will focus on removing and rescuing people in unhealthy family systems from their survival roles. We will also learn more about the redemption process of the central addicts. It's impossible to fix anything unless you realize it is broken. Just the same, once you see the brokenness, you may find it overwhelming to know how to make it right.

The families won't be able to use any personal efforts to change the system. The system that has been aligned with a faulty center has only one solution—to have that center removed and replaced by the Spirit of God. Because human beings naturally resist change, this is usually a long-term process. However, we *have* seen families transition this center point fairly quickly. It depends on two variables: where the family is right now and how much each member is willing to move toward a new center based on Christ Jesus.

We will be looking at the principles of intervention next, but for now, take some time to embrace your own family's homeostasis roles.

Application Points

1. Explain what your role was/is in the crisis mode of addiction.

_____
_____
_____
_____

2. What was your role as a child in your own family system? Can you see any similarities?

_____
_____
_____
_____

3. What have your emotions displayed during this crisis?

_____
_____
_____
_____

4. Can you define any behaviors that were used to gain control or to cope?

_____
_____
_____
_____

5. Write down anything negative happening inside you right now. This could include depression, anxiety, fear, anger, resentment and any other feelings. Be as honest as possible.

_____
_____
_____
_____

6. Personalize the chart in this chapter and see if you can identify an overall pattern of control. If you feel your family is centered on Christ, state it accordingly.

_____
_____
_____
_____

CHAPTER 7

Intervention

When the family has been entwined in the addiction-centered dynamic, finding an end to it can be complex. Trying to control, mandate or make an addict stop bad behavior won't work. In fact, most families have exhausted every avenue of trying to convince the active addict to stop using. Or, in some cases, the family has even stopped seeking resources and adapted to the addiction as a normal way of life. Still others simply give up and leave, never to return or be involved with the addict again.

You are most likely reading this material because you want to see changes and you believe God can bring healing. Learning how to intervene appropriately in the addict's or BCAP's life can be a difficult task. That's because authentic intervention requires two realities: (1) real love for the person under the influence, and (2) hatred of the addictive behavior itself. If either is compromised, intervention is impossible.

Some family members love the person in an *un*healthy way, thus allowing the addiction and making excuses that support further use. We call this *enabling,* and we will discuss this in detail later. Other family members begin to hate the person under the influence of addiction. Deep resentment drives them to punish the addict or inflict injury onto them. This creates a rebellious atmosphere that, by default, makes intervention unwelcome. It can also end the relationship altogether.

For authentic intervention to occur, an atmosphere must be created that allows God to orchestrate redemption and deters the sinful stronghold of addictive behaviors. Learning how to develop this can be the challenge of a lifetime. Truthfully, we as humans have proven our inability—even with our advanced healthcare system—to overcome addiction. We need a power that is greater than the addiction and greater than our effort; we need God's power to intervene.

In order for the Lord to be welcomed into the scene of our own dynamics, we must first seek to understand His heart and methods of intervention. In other words, if *He* were dealing with an addict, what would He do? From there, we can gain tools to help us know how to apply His wisdom in our own situation with the addict. But we must not expect a "how-to" list to fix our situations. God doesn't operate through a behavioral modification program. He is a *Heart Transformer*—He needs full access both to remove what is not of Him and to inject His own life and resources into the needs of the family.

God's Intervention: The Prodigal Son

The best way to gain access into God's intervention style is to read an example directly from His Word. The story of the prodigal son provides a deeply insightful look into the heart of God. It tells of a loving father who honored his son's right to make choices. This son had asked for his entire share of the inheritance so he could have his freedom and live life *his* way. Truthfully, this request was foolish, perhaps even disrespectful. But despite that, the father honored his request and did not hold him back from receiving his portion at that time.

God obviously places a high value on freedom to use such a radical example. That's because it is a hallmark representation of God's system. Therefore, knowing full well the son would probably fail, the father offered the gift of choice.

As the Prodigal ventured into foolish and careless living, the father didn't chase him down. He didn't issue him an "I-told-you-so" statement. Nor did he join the son's world and try to make him stop. The father's own centering remained intact. Instead, he released his son and let him face the ramifications of his own choices. However, the father most likely actively prayed for his son—waiting and anticipating his return.

When the son wasted his inheritance and faced an enormous famine, he began to grow weary. His poor choices had few benefits, and he was degraded to the point of serving pigs and eating pig food. The pain of his choices became very real. In that broken place, the son carried inside him the knowledge of the place he knew as home. His father hadn't forsaken him; he forsook his father. As he meditated on his horrible circumstances, he resolved he'd rather return home even if it meant assuming a mere servant's status. The pain he experienced in that moment prompted him to yearn to be made well again. The Bible says he had a "come-to-his-senses" moment. This was where his pain awakened him to the reality that he needed help. Finally, at the point of nothingness and brokenness, the son bit his pride, got up and returned home.

While all this happened, the father's love remained. The father continued to love his son in bad choices, never removing his designated position as a son. In fact, his son had a permanent position in his home, not based on the son's behavior, but based on the father's unconditional love toward him. We might picture the son's room being untouched while he was gone—like a hotel room waiting for its new occupant to arrive.

As the story goes, the father caught a glimpse of his precious son from a distance, venturing to return home. Without hesitation or the slightest resistance, he ran to greet his son with open arms and placed a ring on his finger to symbolize honor. The father even went as far as to throw a party in honor of his son's return.

The significant thing to know here is that the son's return represented the act of *repentance.* The son didn't just physically return to a physical home, but he spiritually returned to a God-base. Since this was the father's main concern and prayer, there was great celebration when it did happen. It was the answer for which he had been longing.

Applying Principles

While the prodigal son is likely a parable we've heard repeatedly, it provides distinct revelation regarding intervention. These principles will help us better understand how we can effectively develop our own intervention.

- **The father's homeostatic family system was based on freedom.** Members could come and go. They had the right to make choices even if they were wrong. The contrast of this would be a control-based system. It would have tried to restrain the son. As a result, the son most likely would have rebelled.

- **The father's love didn't depend on behaviors; he loved even in sin and brokenness.** Wrong choices didn't sway the father's heart of deep, steadfast love for his son. Yet his love didn't condone wrongful behaviors, either. The Prodigal's wrong choices hurt the father deeply but didn't change the status of their relationship. Contrast this with an unhealthy family system where love is often skewed or lacking. There might have been a door slammed on the Prodigal Son, disowning him because of his negative choices. Love would have been offered again only after it had been "earned." Or, the father could have loved his son in an unhealthy way and entered into an enabling role.

- **The father allowed the son's choices to take root—he didn't have to follow him or track him down and get him to see his choices were wrong.** That the father remained at home is a very telling revelation of God's heart. God will not hover, hunt and force our return to Him. A contrast to the father's actions would have been the father's obsession to rescue his son or find out what he was doing. If this had happened, the father would have begun to center his life around his son's problems. He would have entered the insane roller-coaster of his son's behavior. His attempt at control would have only pushed the son further away.

- **The father never tried to intercept the natural consequences of a bad choice.** As we will discuss in greater detail, God loves us enough to let our bad choices hurt. They become teachable moments. In this story, the father had to endure his own pain as he was watching and waiting. The contrast of this would have been the father rescuing his son from the "come-to-his-senses" moment. Imagine the father bringing grapes, cheese and soft pillows into the pigpen. Imagine the father paying for an apartment to "rescue" him from his awful living environment. Had this occurred, the son would have had no incentive to return home. The story would not have ended in redemption.

- **The father's heart remained pure and clear from resentment.** He was most concerned about his son's well-being and the overall condition of his heart. He knew his son would have to learn lessons on his own. Had the father harbored deep bitterness and resentment, his own heart would have become sick. He would have not only carried the problems of his son but would also have lost his own freedom. Resentment makes the heart sick as nothing else can.

- **The father endured through faith and hope.** While we aren't given the specifics, the picture of the father awaiting his son's return most likely represents the father's faith that his son *would* come home. When faith and hope are removed, deep depression and discouragement can plague us. Through faith, the centering point rests more on God's ability than on the bad choices of the addict.

- **The father was never ashamed of his son—there wasn't the slightest thread of shame in his approach to his son's return.** In fact, it was quite the opposite. The father honored the son's choice to return. This showed the father placed a higher stake on redemption than on the initial sin. Had there been shame, the father would have been embarrassed by his son's return. He would have dishonored him and subjected him to the status of a servant. The family would have functioned under the toxic dynamic of a *shame-based system* where wrongs outweigh and have more force than forgiveness. No one could have been free.

The Other Brother Mentality

While the father was healthy, the story displays a brother who had taken on an adaptive role. This brother wasn't quite as happy about the Prodigal's return. There's a good chance he had to accommodate his brother's absence by making up for things the Prodigal wasn't there to do. In his own mind, he reasoned that good behavior should have been honored, and bad behavior considered shameful to the family name. But ironically, and very astonishingly, the father did just the opposite. He honored repentance and didn't reward good behavior. Not that he didn't appreciate the "good" brother, but this brother's mind-set was missing the father's very own heart. Let's see what the Word of God says about the older brother's struggle:

> "The older brother was angry and wouldn't go in. His father came out and begged him, but he replied, 'All these years I've slaved for you and never once refused to do a single thing you told me to. And in all that time you never gave me even one young goat for a feast with my friends. Yet when this son of yours comes back after squandering your money on prostitutes, you celebrate by killing the fattened calf!'

> "His father said to him, 'Look, dear son, you have always stayed by me, and everything I have is yours. We had to celebrate this happy day. For your brother was dead and has come back to life! He was lost, but now he is found!'" (Luke 15: 28–32)

God rewards repentance and brokenness and seeks redemption as His primary agenda. When repentance occurs, a celebration takes place. Self-improvement (cleaning up for God) does not motivate God—He is moved by humility and godly contrition.

The older brother's dilemma is understandable and is one of the many facets of God's character that goes beyond our human understanding. As with the brother, you are certainly entitled to your own struggles about what occurred. You may have a difficult time rewarding repentance or feel you deserve to be honored for the work and constraints the addict's lifestyle caused. However, it is clear that God encourages those on the "other side" of someone's bad behavior to affirm and celebrate their return.

But the father didn't merely scold the older brother for a wrongful mind-set; instead, he expressed loving affirmation. The father knew the son's point of view was flawed, yet he understood the enormous difficultly the son had in processing the situation. To be honest, it made no human sense!

God's response is one that all family members should take note of. God told the older son *he already possessed the inheritance and security of being his son.* He wasn't lost like the Prodigal. In other words, the older brother was *already living out the reward of being a faithful son.*

Be encouraged, families, that God wants to validate and honor you as His child as much as the addict who needs to return. But that validation may come in another form. God understands and loves you not for what you've *done* but because *you are His.* He wants to be sure we understand His purposes operate through grace, not effort. If He were to reward self-effort, He would be minimizing the need for the cross.

If you find your heart resisting the principle of God's grace, you—or any family member—can lay yourself before God and say, "Help me, Lord. I can't do this. I can't think or respond as You would! I return my entire being into Your care." This motivates the heart of God as nothing else can.

A Prayer of Repentance

Wherever I have been, on the road of rebellion or attempting to be the "Good One," I need help. Lord God, this life isn't about me. It isn't formed around what I can or can't do right. It's built around the fact that You have a room reserved in Your heart for me and I belong to You. I want to return there if I've left or gone astray. If someone I love has left, I ask that You teach me to wait, to pray and to anticipate their return. Help me rely on Your tools, not my own. Help me see the power and precious resources of pain. Furthermore, give me a heart filled with a redemptive understanding. Help me remain humble and teachable and willing to allow You to love me as I am. Please protect _____ from danger and harm other than for it to be used to draw them back to You.

In Jesus' name, amen.

Tools of Intervention

In our own dealings with addiction, none of us will do it perfectly. Family members do many things out of survival mode (see Chapter 6)—and most of them have good intentions. But their efforts are equivalent to trying to come against a full-force hurricane. As the storm is breaking everything apart, family members are clinging to the broken pieces and trying to glue things back together. Thus, their efforts fail, and their hope of healing plunges.

The way God wants to enter the scene of addiction is entirely different from our own attempts. The insanity of trying to repair a broken house while it is being ripped apart must be swallowed up by one reality: *God can!* Yes, it is impossible for us. Yes, we will fail. But God will not fail! He reigns above the furious storm. He has resources that can speak "stop" in the middle of the storm. These are different from our own resources, however, and therefore we must be equipped with understanding.

Using basic principles we have established through the Prodigal Son in God's Word, we are now ready to develop new tools—tools that reflect His heart. And even more important, tools that will put Him in charge. We must understand—God's way leads us to create an environment that lets Him intervene and cease the storm. We can do nothing directly to change a person's heart. In many ways, it's easier to feel we're in control and can assist and stop the addict. Thus, learning to respond via *God's* intervention method requires inner work in our hearts. This is why recovery is needed for all family members, not just the person struggling with addiction.

#1. A Full Surrender Must Occur where Family Members Acknowledge their Inability to Change the Addict

Family members must see the storm and face the fact they cannot conquer its power. *This is perhaps the most important step of any.* As we see in the story of the prodigal, the father lived in a position of surrender. Freedom allows the gift of choice. God cannot operate where we are attempting to control. When we release the addict to Him, we give Him permission to use His strategies. We get out of the way and allow the God of the universe to intervene.

Surrender sounds easy as a solution written in black and white. However, it needs to occur in the heart. It is not easy to surrender when you have maintained a sense of control. It will be something you must individually work out between the Father and yourself.

True surrender occurs when we stop looking to manage outcomes. This means we release any effort to manipulate how the addict thinks, feels or makes choices. It means we entrust their needs to Him, and we officially "fire ourselves" from any direct management role. That won't mean we do nothing; it means whatever we do will be under God's mandate, not our personal efforts.

A Prayer to Surrender
Lord God,

I struggle with release because I know no other way. I have done everything possible to manage and deal with the problems of my family. I have carried the weight of responsibility, including trying to love, even though it wasn't done in the proper context. It seems that surrender means I have lost the battle. But in trust, I'm not willing to give up. I'm giving it to You. I acknowledge that You are worthy to meet the needs of _____. I admit to You that I can't. I humble myself before You and ask You to do for us what we cannot do for ourselves. Come into our situation and be our God.

In Jesus' name, amen.

#2. Declare Your Love toward the Person under the Influence

Love wants the addict freed from the bondage of addiction. Love isn't condoning the behavior or helping the addict when they make bad choices. It is common for family members to be disillusioned about how to love. There are many reasons for this. If you are angry or feel the need to punish the addict, your own heart needs to be healed. Otherwise, when you move forward in any form of intervention, you might inflict injury into the process. That doesn't mean your pain is not legitimate. It absolutely is. But you will need a separate process inside your own heart to deal with this.

#3. Understand the Purpose of Pain

Back in Chapter 3, we learned that addiction distorted the purpose of pain. Rather than use pain to deal with its source, the addict medicates over it and copes with pain by not facing it. But the wound that produced the pain never left. And more and more layers are created in the process. Pain, therefore, will be needed, as it was in the case of the Prodigal Son, for the real drive of addiction to be understood.

Pain is not bad. It has a blessed purpose. Pain asks us to get help. In fact, all recovery is based on the addict's ability to face pain. If this has not yet happened, you need to learn to partner with God and allow the pain to do its perfect work. Here are some highlights from His Word to assist, but there are many, many more:

> Now I am glad I sent it, not because it hurt you, but because the pain caused you to repent and change your ways. It was the kind of sorrow God wants his people to have, so you were not harmed by us in any way. (2 Corinthians 7:9)

> No discipline is enjoyable while it is happening—it's painful! But afterward there will be a peaceful harvest of right living for those who are trained in this way. (Hebrews 12:11)

#4. All Forms of Enabling the Addiction Must End

At a very basic level, *enabling* is a system that is created that unknowingly promotes addictive behavior. It does this by allowing it or cushioning any negative consequences that should be the natural effect of poor choices. Enabling reinforces bad behavior while offering no reward for positive change. It ends up doing the exact opposite of what is necessary—it allows the addiction and hurts the addict.

That's not to say that family members can't ever assist the addict. Certainly, there is a time and place, especially when we understand the extreme bondage they are under. But that "help" must support the addict's recovery, not help them function comfortably in the addiction itself.

The most common forms of enabling come in very subtle and disguised forms. These may include the following:

- **Removing the consequences of the addict's bad behavior.** This means a family member removes the consequence altogether rather than allowing the addict to deal with the reality of a bad choice. Jeff kept spending money to support his habit. While his mother was aware of his addiction, she continued to be manipulated. When he couldn't pay his rent or afford to buy his favorite concert ticket, Jeff's mom paid it for him. Jeff had no motivation to quit. He had the best of both worlds.
- **Continuing to own the addict's problems rather than allowing them to own their own problems.** Family members are sometimes more concerned about the addict's situation than the addict is. In the addiction cycle, addicts are oftentimes numbed and unaware of the complete chaos and insanity they create. When Julie received a drunk-driving ticket and

was put in jail, her mother was hysterical. She drove four hours to claim Julie's car, have it towed and repaired and post bail money. As Julie came out of jail, she was disrespectful and rude and had no appreciation for her mom's efforts. She immediately went drinking while her mother secured an expensive lawyer to bail her out of her bad choices. Julie didn't need to own her problems because her mother carried them for her.

- **Allowing the addict's denial to dictate reality.** Denial is a powerful force that demands everyone to respond to it. Rather than deal with addiction, denial forces members to view it through the addict's perspective. Tom's addiction was ruling the home as he terrorized the family with all the things they were doing wrong. The focus and blame was continually placed on them throughout the day, giving Tom permission to continue to use. The family obliged and agreed with him, thus helping perpetuate that denial. That's because they were too afraid and beaten down to come against Tom. Outside help was needed for them as well as for Tom.

- **Filling in the gaps for everything the addict can't or won't do.** While the addict can do irresponsible things, they usually are failing to do their God-given duty. From work to home, the addict often doesn't need to fulfill their role *because someone else is already doing it for them.* Marilyn worked two jobs to support her husband. He had no ambition to find a job and said he was entitled to be at home. He lived off the benefits of his wife's income while offering very little in return. Marilyn did everything for her husband, and he had no incentive to learn to carry his weight or stop his addiction. Marilyn unknowingly created adaptation that perpetuated rather than ended the addiction cycle.

- **Excusing the addict's behavior, blaming something or someone else.** When a family supports the addict's behavior, they will actually look for ways to protect the addict from even having to *admit* a problem. In fact, this is the most common error parents and close family members make. In their own idea of "love," they see "a good heart" underneath the addict and don't ever deal with the wrongful behavior. This protection can become so extreme that if anything or anyone threatens that person, the family can actually lie and manipulate in the same way as the addict. Frank was in denial over his wife's problem and didn't want to do anything that would hurt or disrupt her. Thus, when people tried to convince him to get help for her, he was defensive. He excused and justified her behavior even to the point of lying and covering for her. In doing so, he was protecting the very bondage she was under. He was serving her addiction every bit as much as she was.

Usually, when the addict reaches the end of their resources and feels the pain, they are ready to cry "help!" Again, this is not guaranteed, but when the negative effects of addiction far outweigh the benefits, the addict often wants assistance. At first, however, a war might break out. If the addict is accustomed to having their needs met—but now those needs aren't accommodated—the response could be quite volatile. *You should always seek outside assistance if violence or excessive threats could potentially harm you or the addict.* It's also important to make adjustment in the tone of love, not shame. In fact, if shame is present, it must first be dealt with before healthy intervention can occur.

Some scenarios where addiction becomes intolerable and produces more pain than benefit include the following:

- Addict is forced to feel ramifications of bad choices. This means his or her own decisions cause problems, and no one is available to remove those consequences.
- Addict deals with overwhelming loss because of lifestyle and choices. Oftentimes, everything the addict once loved or valued begins to slip away.
- Addict faces a potential marriage loss. A spouse may tolerate the addiction up to a certain point and then opt to leave the marriage.
- Addict faces the potential of a job loss. The addict may lose functionality and can't function at work. Since places of employment are, in most circumstances, required to accommodate substance abuse treatment, this doesn't need to occur. But, sadly, it can when the addict isn't willing to get help. (Learn more about the Americans with Disabilities Act [ADA] and the Family and Medical Leave Act [FMLA].)
- Addict faces serious health problems. The physical body can be worn down and sick, resulting in serious health issues or even potential death.
- Addict faces serious criminal and legal problems. Both jail and prison can be the "come-to-the- senses" moment.
- Addict has a spiritual encounter—conviction by the Holy Spirit. It's possible for an addict to hear a message or read the Word and receive conviction directly from the Holy Spirit.

As we look at this list, one thing should be clear: pain is a necessary ingredient. What may seem "unloving"—trusting in God (not our own efforts) and *allowing these breaking points*—are actually the most loving acts we can offer. That's because the addict needs the toxic addiction released like a literal chain. The addict is blinded to addiction and serving it. But underneath is a precious person you love, a person who has the opportunity to live, love and be free.

Does this have a risk? Of course. Addiction does kill. That's why help, when wanted, should always be offered to the struggling addict—as long as it aligns with the addict's sobriety and healing. But when the addict is in denial, the most loving action is *not* to participate in the addict's unhealthy choices to continue to use drugs or alcohol. This may result in severing the relationship for a season or putting it on hold until help is sought. Doing so places a healthy standard (*boundary*) on the relationship. It lets the addict know you are absolutely committed to their well-being and will absolutely not condone the lifestyle of addiction. *It's always important to express love as a motivator.*

#5. Actively Pray and Seek God for Their Return

Surrender and the removal of enabling may be a stark contrast for a family member who has been caring for the addict hands-on. The most important change, however, will not be a totally passive role. Rather, the active role of the family member seeking intervention will revolve around prayer and supplication. While this process may be intended for the addict, it will bring radical transformation to the family member as well. That's because prayer creates a dialogue that begins to assert God's authority. It creates a dependency on Him and thus moves our own centering point to Him. This will have enormous ramifications. Family members will be able to experience God, to know Him and to begin to absorb His character. They will begin to experience personal change and the ability to see themselves and others through His perspective. This will be a process and will be discussed in detail in Chapter 11.

#6. Place a Holy Standard (Boundary) that Protects Your Own Heart from Wrongful Behaviors

The story of the Prodigal Son is one of healthy boundaries yet the adherence of personal rights. The father gave his son his own rights without hindrance. In the same manner, he allowed his son his own consequences without interference. While the family system is meant to unite the members, this is meant to occur under a formula of love, respect, intimacy, acceptance, grace and holiness. Each person within a healthy family system is validated in their unique right to think, to feel, to make choices and to engage with God and one another. Wrong choices that hurt another must bear a consequence of some sort. That consequence is meant to validate the sacredness of the person(s) affected. We see this mentality in our legal system. If we break the law, we will face a penalty. The governance of boundaries in a healthy way isn't to control but to protect.

Boundaries also allow family members to live lives centered on God rather than on addiction. Through boundaries, family members can bar addictive behavior and set consequences for wrongful choices that attempt to sabotage their hearts.

Boundaries will include the following:
- The opportunity for the addict to be free to make choices (not be controlled).
- The communicated standard of allowance in the home (what is okay, what is not okay). This standard can't dictate someone else's behavior (which would be control). Rather, it acts as a protective fence that determines what is given access.
- A clearly designated and reasonable consequence ("if you drink, this will happen").
- A willingness to follow through on the consequence. If consequences are not enforced, the boundary no longer has any value.
- A loving intent to allow the addict to repent and return at any point and be welcomed with open arms when recovery occurs.
- A loving intent not to be manipulated when the addict wants to return under any other circumstances (blames the program, blames treatment, says they don't need help and offer similar responses).

#7. Implement a Personal Intervention Plan

Intervention should occur when the addict is in active addiction. The plan can be written before a relapse occurs as a form of prevention and planning (See Chapter 12). If the addict has never sought help for addiction, you will need to form this plan with a recovery leader, pastor, professional interventionist, counselor or some other helper. We have provided some guidelines, but seeking the advice from others who understand is essential. *Do not take matters in your own hands!*

Preparing for Intervention

When you are dealing with an addict who has toxic behaviors, suddenly ceasing the ways you have enabled him or her is not enough. A healthy intervention will also allow the addict to make good choices that can potentially lead to freedom and recovery. God is the true author of intervention, thus the practical steps merely establish an environment where He is allowed to bring break through.

For example, Paula was ready to intervene with her adult son Peter. She had recognized the ways she had encouraged his addiction and wanted to stop. However, cutting him off without any a positive alternative to his current lifestyle would have been unfair. Therefore, Paula developed a plan. She began to highlight how she had been enabling, and recognized that she was no longer willing to participate. While she saw her part, she also realized she could not help Peter, and her son needed outside support. Therefore, she sought to find resources for him. Paula researched several programs in her area that she felt was a good match for Peter.

In preparing for an intervention, Paula wrote out the things she was no longer willing to accept. With the help of a recovery leader, Paula was able to meet with Peter and highlight her concerns. She expressed her love for him rather than merely blaming and criticizing his wrong-doing. Because she understood the nature of addiction, she was determined that she could love Peter, but hate his addiction. Therefore, she showed compassion but firmness. The recovery leader had Paula read Peter a letter that expressed what she was no longer willing to support while he was actively using. This included:

- Living in her home rent-free
- Paying his bills
- Offering him daily support with household responsibility

She had enabled Peter for so long, she recognized that in some ways she participated in his lifestyle. Therefore a major change of events needed to happen. In Paula's case, she opted for an extended treatment program and then required that he remain in sober living for several months to help develop life skills and become self-supporting. If Peter wasn't willing, she would ask him to move out of the family home. This had a steep consequence for both as her greatest fear was losing her son or seeing him suffer. It took the strength and support of Jesus and others to help make that decision.

Families make different choices when deciding to intervene. An intervention is no guarantee, and if boundaries aren't stated in a loving, respectful and redemptive-oriented manner, it will merely turn into a fight. Guilt triggers are pushed by the addict, and many times families back down.

Sometimes intervention isn't quite so simple. When a wife, for example, is being financially supported, an intervention dealing with her husband's addictive behavior may lead to consequences that will be very inconvenient for her. This is why some family members opt to live with addiction; they feel it's a better alternative than losing the relationship altogether. No one can make that decision for you. Like the addict, you will need to be ready to be serious about boundaries and intervention. A plan is meaningless unless it is adhered to.

If the intervention is successful, getting addicts to agree to get help is only the beginning. They will often resist the process in various ways if they don't feel truly ready (this is covered in Chapter 12). Some are willing to get detox help, but then will convince the family they don't need further help. Others will insist on being medicated in other ways. If the addict doesn't want help, it's best to simply withdraw, set the boundary, and then allow him or her the opportunity to get help when ready. If you allow them to live without any direct negative consequences, there is little chance they will seek help (this is the concept of allowing the addict to "come to his senses").

If the addict is so severely dangerous he or she may be suicidal, then forcing help may be necessary. This is not usually the case, but it should be pointed out in the event this is possible. When threats of suicide occur, take them serious by calling the local emergency line. If they are being used as a threat, it's better to follow through on that threat than risk further harm. *If violence is occurring, you must seek help immediately. Take each threat or act of violence as if your life depends on it. There are hotlines and domestic violence shelters that can help.*

The addict may be offered several choices in a recovery plan. All this depends upon the level of support that is required and the accessibility to services. When someone *wants* help, there is usually always a means, but some research is needed. Finding these options should occur *before* a formal intervention.

Getting the Addict Sober

Many addicts feel that if they can get sober, it should be enough. But as we will learn in Chapter 8, mere sobriety is not the goal. A transformation process must take place to assure that the addiction will not continue or be transferred to something else. The first step of an intervention is to find a supportive place where a person can physically be released from the effects of the drug or alcohol. This is called drug or alcohol detoxification. This can happen in a hospital, professional residential facility or with a trusted friend (not recommended for dangerous detoxification processes).

Finding Recovery

Recovery happens when the internal work and heart transformation can be processed (See Chapter 8). This can take place in a variety of settings, and it should be the individual's choice. Some of the recovery choices include:

- *Alcoholics Anonymous or Narcotics Anonymous (AA/NA) Recovery groups with sponsor —* These meetings are offered in virtually every city in America. At these meetings, addicts can find a sponsor. However, they do not promote Jesus Christ specifically, rather allow people to select a "Higher Power." Some addicts get clean and remain sober in this setting, but if chronic relapse occurs, it may not be enough.
- *Celebrate Recovery groups with sponsor —* The advantage of Celebrate Recovery is that it uses the 12-steps in a Biblical manner, and allows and edifies people to engage in a relationship with Jesus Christ. Like AA, it can be sufficient, but some people will need more structured support in the beginning phases.
- *Outpatient Programs —* Outpatient addiction programs can offer support and accountability, along with counseling and classes. They often allow people to continue to live at home. This can have both advantages and disadvantages depending on the circumstances.

/74

- *Sober housing* — A sober home merely provides a safe place of accountability, but it does not actually provide any recovery. This is a good option, but needs to come alongside a separate recovery plan.
- *Rehab/Treatment Programs with Housing* — Intensive programs include housing and are far more structured. They typically include a team of professionals who understand the nature of addiction. The benefit is that they take addicts away from their environment and allow them time to process through their issues individually. It also provides the family with time to further work through a recovery and boundary plan. These programs can range from no-cost ministries to very high dollar luxury environments. What should be sought is the *content* of the program, and the goals of the treatment process.

Again, developing an intervention plan doesn't assure it will work. Families must be committed to the "what if" side of an intervention. This means if the addict either doesn't agree, or enters into the program but then relapses, what will happen? In the case of sobriety, we have included a family planning section in Chapter 12 to work through this process in detail. That plan is written once the addict *agrees* to recovery.

While the practical side is important, we must not forget what the majority of this chapter entailed: the method and condition by which the heart gets broken and brought back into a relationship with the Father.

If you have a Prodigal in your life, they are following their affections. The prodigal son ventured for the pleasure he believed resided in an outside place. When he chased down those affections, he discovered they were a lie. What he was looking for was really with him all along, he just had not yet accessed or appreciated the reality of the Father's love for him.

It is not your job to change the affections of the addict's heart. However, you can make the affection of the addiction much less attractive, and the benefit of surrendering and returning 'home" appear much more appealing. It won't happen by fixing, changing or preventing the consequences and pain. It will happen by letting the pain have its perfect work. Will you partner with God?

A Prayer of Intervention
Lord God,

How often I have fought and sought advice on how to save. How often I believe that if that problem were resolved, I would also be okay. It is clear that I'm entangled in this process too and that my real need is to become untangled. Show me how to be free from anything that has kept me from seeing clearly. And from there, I ask for wisdom, authentic wisdom, to make decisions that can establish an environment conducive to Your redemption. Please give me wisdom and understanding as to how to develop a plan of intervention. Help me Father! I need You!

In Jesus' name, amen.

Intervention Plan Worksheet

Preparing for an Intervention

Am I ready to pursue an intervention? ☐ Yes ☐ No

Who can I use for a resource?
☐ Christian professional interventionist
☐ Local pastor
☐ Friend/family
☐ Myself

It is recommended you use an outside source when and if possible. It should be someone who has an understanding of the principles covered in this material.

Surrender

Have I surrendered and do I understand I cannot change, fix or make
_____ stop using? ☐ Yes ☐ No
Can I leave the results to God, even if I don't like them? ☐ Yes ☐ No
If no, continue to process through personal recovery program or seek outside support in learning how to let go. It is the hardest part of the entire process and so support is necessary.

Love

Am I motivated by love or retaliation in wanting the addict to get help?
☐ I am motivated by love. I truly want the best for him or her, and thus I am taking action to benefit _____'s well-being.
☐ Right now I'm so angry I don't know if it's love that's motivating, or if I want to make _____ suffer or "wake up".

If you are not motivated by love, continue to work through a personal recovery process. It is understandable to be hurt and experience anger. However, you won't be able to effectively intervene unless you truly want your family member to get better for his or her well-being.

The Purpose of Pain

Am I in touch with pain's purpose or have I tried to protect and prevent it? Am I ready to let pain work?
☐ No, I am not interested in allowing _____ to face pain.
☐ Yes, I am willing to let pain have its way
If you find yourself struggling, you are not alone. Again, your own support system is essential.

Ending Enabling:

Identify in detail the ways you have been enabling based on what you learned:

_____
_____
_____
_____
_____
_____
_____
_____
_____

Prayer

Are you actively praying and seeking God? ☐ Yes ☐ No
If no, can you commit to it daily? ☐ Yes ☐ No

Boundaries

The formal plan of intervention is nothing more than a boundary. A boundary sets guidelines about your own willingness or unwillingness to participate in someone else's choices. A boundary does not control someone else's behavior, but rather states what is allowed or not allowed. Please review the principles of a boundary as discussed in this chapter. With that information, write out some formalized boundary requests.

What I'm not willing to allow concerning your addiction:
_____
_____
_____
_____
_____
_____
_____
_____

These are the ways I value you and our relationship:
_____
_____
_____
_____
_____
_____
_____
_____

This is how your addiction changes that:
_____

_____
_____
_____
_____
_____
_____
_____

I feel you need help. I'm not longer willing to live with the behavior of addiction. If you don't want to change, this is what I need to do for the sake of you and our relationship:

_____
_____
_____
_____
_____
_____
_____
_____

If this cannot happen, I will need to take the following action:

_____
_____
_____
_____
_____
_____
_____

Write a separate letter that expresses the heart and real feelings. Be loving, not condemning. Encourage and support when and if possible.

_____
_____
_____
_____
_____
_____
_____

Intervention Criteria

For substance addiction (or other addictions), a plan should include specific steps and a specific option immediately should help be agreed upon.

The following options are being made available to you (check those that apply):
I am willing to support the following options:

☐ Detox _____

☐ Sober Living _____ Length: _____

☐ Treatment _____ Length: _____

☐ You need to enter into this agreement on (date) _____

☐ I will support you financially

☐ I cannot support you financially

If you don't agree to help, the following steps will be taken:

_____
_____
_____
_____
_____
_____
_____
_____
_____

When you are ready and willing to get help, I would like to be in a relationship with you. This is what my heart feels about that.

_____
_____
_____
_____
_____
_____
_____
_____
_____

CHAPTER 8

The Hope of Redemption

When Jesus came to walk on the earth, He was fully aware of its condition. Like walking onto the scene of wreckage after a storm, He felt the despair of what was broken. He didn't expect things to be right, beautiful or whole. In fact, like a disaster relief expert, His very reason for being here was to fix and redeem the ravaged storm site.

The Word of God introduces us to this radical, loving and gracious Jesus who had no expectations, no self-needs to satisfy and no imposed criteria for His involvement other than an invitation. We are told in the book of John that He did not come to judge the world but to save it (John 3:17). Therefore, He didn't expect to find people in a righteous state and most certainly didn't merely chastise them for their own heart's condition. The Jesus of the Bible stooped down, entered the mess and met people directly at their point of need. For those who received Him, He was able to dissolve brokenness and orchestrate a powerful reordering. Wherever His life and power were injected, everything was made new. The price He paid at Calvary bore everything necessary to bring things back to life.

That same Jesus is alive and well and residing inside us through the Holy Spirit (if we have invited Him). Understanding His agenda and overall nature puts our own situations into proper perspective. And He waits now to be summoned to the scene of our own storms. Despite the mess, entanglement and damage, He comes with every resource in the power of grace to redeem and restore us at an individual level. However, in God's kingdom, "seeing is *not* believing." Instead, faith requires that we believe *before* we see. Both the addict and family members must learn individually how to connect and relate spiritually to Him through a personal relationship.

It's amazing how many times Jesus comes knocking on the hearts of addicts and family members alike, yet is continually refused entry. Within the stronghold of the addictive system, family members can have an almost compulsive need to problem solve, thus diminishing

God's role. The addict avoids Him altogether.

Yet our merciful God stands ready to be dispatched to rescue, redeem and rebuild. But first, the family and addict must believe He is fully competent. Sometimes this requires a process in the heart.

A Prayer to Invite God

Dear Father,

I hire You. I hire You because You are competent and able. I hire You because I believe You can bring the aid and assistance for my family members and me. I hire You because I don't have the resources. I acknowledge that my own best efforts fall short. Build my hope and trust in You. Give me eyes to see as You see. Fill me with Your Holy Spirit so I can abound and be free to be all You created me to be. Fill me with that freedom so I can encourage and partner with You to see those around me set free. I give You rightful permission to break through the barriers of survival living and to be the God Your Word claims You are—powerful, mighty, loving and merciful. In my weakness, I can be strong in You. I can be everything You created and intended me to be.

In Jesus' name, amen.

What Is Recovery?

All true recovery involves departing the survival lifestyle (via chemical or other faulty adaptations) and building a life centered on Christ. Most who have experienced a Christ-centered recovery process in its fullness would call it the gift of a lifetime. Through recovery, they received something they never had in the first place: authentic love, peace, joy, wholeness and security. These rewards are so massive that people who have received them will claim gratitude for the storm and wrecking that occurred first. For without that they may never have had the opportunity to experience God's rebuilding.

True recovery involves two redemptive motions of God: removal of what doesn't belong (the debris of the storm) and replacement with what He intended (rebuilding after the storm). God doesn't modify behaviors. He's not concentrating on making external changes alone. That's because all true change must occur by resolving the deep-rooted issues that affect the soul and spirit. Trying to change behaviors without changing the heart first is like building a structure minus a sturdy foundation. The wall and roof would eventually fall down. But when God is given access, He builds from the ground up—beginning with a foundation that is strong and dependable and can house the very life of God.

While transferring systems may seem an obvious goal, change is naturally resisted. The homeostasis environment that has been created, individually and within the family system, tends to seek its faulty centering point. In reality, change is a difficult journey. Seasons of transition can be filled with both fear and hope. There is no magic fix to instantly zap everything into place—not that God's touch isn't profound. One touch of His Spirit can set in motion a brand new life. But much of recovery is a *process* of change. It can at times be painful and other times glorious. It does require a lifelong commitment to follow Him and allow Him to recenter our lives. But here we start to escape the power of the storm and move into the wonderful reality of life in Christ.

Anyone who has experienced the authentic power of God's love will find abiding in Him to be exceedingly abundantly beyond anything they ever thought or imagined (Ephesians 3:20). He is not a religion. He is not merely a history book. He is a Person—a Lover, Healer, Redeemer, Father, Spouse and Friend. The journey will never be about sobriety alone—the goal is to know Him, be conquered by His love and be conformed to His image.

Framing Christian Addiction Recovery

While we will review recovery for all family members, the next few chapters will deal with the recovery process of the addict. It can be tough to understand how to incorporate Christianity into a process hijacked by the secular worldview. In truth, there are varied avenues that can comprise a positive recovery program. We certainly can't claim what we will share as the only effective pathway to recovery. However, only Jesus Christ can bring true inner transformation, and therefore we will focus upon His principles.

We believe what the world calls a brain disease is a sin disease. Everything God created was good. But the broken condition of the human heart took that good thing and perverted it into another outcome. By seeing sin rather than merely the physiological as the disease, we can apply a spiritual solution instead of relying fully on the medical system.

Calling addiction a sin problem doesn't mean we will use tactics of guilt and shame. We don't need to beat someone over the head with the Bible. A pastor who exclusively gives biblical justification to the sinful nature of addiction often negates or misunderstands bondage. This can promote a very callous and misinformed approach to aiding the addict. Everything in this world done apart from God will lead to some form of death within. Addiction is one of many ways this can occur.

On the other hand, we are not ignorant of the disease model embraced by secular and many Christian organizations. We use medical professionals in our program, and at times certain medication is necessary. But we simply refuse to stand under the world's authoritative label. God can deliver a person from the "disease" of addiction because He already paid the price for it. But recovery must be a lifelong commitment. And for the addict, this must entail a serious, diligent and continual pursuit of change.

Are the Twelve Steps Biblical?

Nearly everyone is familiar with the 12-step programs. Before we delve into a deeper form of biblical deliverance, we want to briefly touch on this type of program. The twelve steps have a rich heritage in Christianity. The men who formed Alcoholics Anonymous (AA) had a spiritual conversion to Christ and believed He was the solution entirely. However, through time and changes the program focused more and more on respecting individual beliefs in a "higher power." In some ways, this was necessary. Some people aren't ready for a Christian approach and wouldn't seek help at all unless this option were available. The process itself is effective enough to bring a form of stabilization. Most people don't know that those steps are actually pointing to God's system of redemption. They are twelve biblical steps (See page 84) that offer a spiritual prescription of Scripture.

People benefit from the twelve steps even if they don't know Jesus. These steps are

The 12 Steps and the Bible

Step One - "We admitted that we were powerless over our alcohol, that our lives had become unmanageable".	And I know that nothing good lives in me, that is, in my sinful nature. I want to do what is right, but I can't. 1Romans 7:18 18
Step Two - "Came to believe that a power greater than our-selves could restore us to sanity".	But you will receive power when the Holy Spirit comes upon you. And you will be my witnesses, telling people about me everywhere—in Jerusalem, throughout Judea, in Samaria, and to the ends of the earth." Acts 1:8
Step Three - "Made a decision to turn our will and our lives over to the care of God as we understood him".	If you confess with your mouth that Jesus is Lord and believe in your heart that God raised him from the dead, you will be saved. Scripture - Romans 10:9
Step Four - "Made a searching and fearless moral inventory of ourselves".	Search me, O God, and know my heart; test me and know my anxious thoughts.Point out anything in me that offends you, and lead me along the path of everlasting life. Psalm 139:23-24
Step Five - "We admitted to God, to ourselves, and to another human being the exact nature of our wrongs".	But if we confess our sins to him, he can be depended on to forgive us and to cleanse us from every wrong. – 1 John 1:9 If we say that we have no sin, we are only fooling ourselves and refusing to accept the truth. Scripture – 1 John 1:8 Confess your sins to each other and pray for each other so that you may be healed. Scripture – James 6:15
Step Six - "We became entirely ready to have God remove all these defects of character".	Humble yourselves before the Lord, and He will lift you up in honor. – James 4:10
Step Seven - "We humbly asked Him to remove our shortcom-ings".	But if we confess our sins to him, he can be depended on to forgive us and to cleanse us from every wrong. – 1 John 1:9
Step Eight - "Made a list of all persons we had harmed, and became willing to make amends to them all".	Do to others as you would like them to do to you.– 1Luke 6:31
Step Nine - "We made direct amends to such people whenever possible, except when to do so would injure them or others".	So if you are presenting a sacrifice at the altar in the Temple and you suddenly remember that someone has something against you, leave your sacrifice there at the altar. Go and be reconciled to that person. Then come and offer your sacrifice to God.– Matt 5:23
Step Ten - "We continued to take personal inventory, and when we were wrong promptly admitted it".	If you think you are standing strong, be careful not to fall. The temptations in your life are no different from what others experience. – 1 Cor. 10:12-13
Step Eleven - "Sought through prayer and meditation to im-prove our conscious contact with God as we understood him, praying only for knowledge of his will for us and the power to carry that out	Let the message about Christ, in all its richness, fill your lives. Teach and counsel each other with all the wisdom He gives. – Col. 3:16
Step Twelve - "Having had a spiritual awakening as a result of these steps, we tried to carry this message to alcoholics, and to practice these principles in all our affairs".	Dear brothers and sisters, if another believer is overcome by some sin, you who are godly should gently and humbly help that person back onto the right path. And be careful not to fall into the same temptation yourself.– Gal. 6:1

actually biblical principles that contain natural benefits. Like laws of nature, these steps work because God designed them to promote a particular change. If you have an addict who resists a Christian approach, it's important that you still embrace the 12-step process. At most meetings at least one or more really do know Jesus and refer to Him as their Higher Power. Sometimes in those meetings, addicts are introduced to their Savior. However, the twelve steps minus God cannot lead to freedom within. There is no freedom or no alignment of identity without a relationship with Jesus Christ. Thus, as wonderful as they are, the twelve steps alone cannot heal the heart—nor can any program. And even more important, they do not save a person for eternity and allow them entrance into God's kingdom.

We won't examine the twelve steps directly but will explain a process connecting people to the power of God's redemptive heart. This process coincides with the twelve steps, and we will show how it aligns with each step. But since we are authoring this book—and administer treatment—through a Spirit-led Christian worldview, we can explain this process in greater detail from God's perspective. We will discuss the need for a 12-step program as a long-term plan and an essential part of the recovery process. It not only contains a remedy, but it also provides a needed community of support.

Understanding Connection

Recovery involves a complete transformation of the person: body, soul and spirit. The body under addiction's bondage needs that influence removed first. The body must deal with cravings and imbalances that have occurred within the brain. *A structured detoxification program is strongly recommended for a safe and effective approach.* The body will need to be cared for through healthy diet and nutrition to make up for the depletions that have occurred. Understanding nutritional needs and supplements is an important aspect of recovery. This book will not address those specific issues. However, we want to emphasize that the physical body's needs cannot be rejected in the name of spiritual healing. Medical help should be sought for any major issues.

The bond to addiction is not just a physical dependency; thus, everything won't simply align when it is gone. Instead, it is a false source of comfort that leads to unthinkable bondage. Addiction empowers the addict with a wrongful set of tools.

Before true change can occur, more than the physical connection must be made. The will must also transfer from a system of selfish, self-centered survival to God-dependency. We learned in Chapter 4 that the spiritual connection with God was broken. This created a disconnect from the Source of life and power. Thus, before learning anything the addict must understand how to reestablish that connection (or connect for the first time).

The Role of the Holy Spirit

The connection needed to perform the deeper work of recovery involves the Person of the Holy Spirit. In fact, He is the source of light, truth, revelation, conviction, comfort, change and eternal hope. It is essential to understand that the Holy Spirit is not "spooky" nor a strange theology. Some people are turned off by His name because they have been exposed to beliefs that seem to make Him perform odd activities. Others don't believe the Holy Spirit is even a present force, citing the Bible as the only necessary entity of the Christian life. While the Bible houses all of God's purposes and promises and instructs us in every single area of life, it was not meant to be read as a novel or "how-to" guide. The Word become flesh and dwelt among us in the form of Jesus Christ (John 1:14). The Bible as a book, in and of itself, cannot change the heart. Even Jesus said:

> "You search the Scriptures because you think they give you eternal life. But the Scriptures point to me! Yet you refuse to come to me to receive this life." (John 5:39–40)

Theology and Bible knowledge won't save a person dying from bondage. In fact, a person can have a head full of biblical truths and a heart completely bankrupt. It's certainly not that the Bible isn't all-sufficient—but rather that the Bible needs to be translated into a relationship with Jesus Christ that will activate the availability of the Holy Spirit. In other words, we need a tangible and authentic power Source that can transform the written Word into an inward reality.

This is the job of the Holy Spirit. The Holy Spirit is a person who has been granted authority in our lives to abide inside us and give us the power to perform God's will. While Jesus saves us and becomes our Bridegroom, the Holy Spirit enters into our lives to align us, make us holy and remove our brokenness. Although they are two different persons, they are also one with the Father (the triune God). Thus, they all have the same power.

Connecting to the Holy Spirit is the most vital step. As an illustration, let's consider the concept of electricity being used in a home. Without this energy source, the use of anything dependent on its power is lost. Those objects needing electricity will still *exist*, but they cannot perform the complex and useful purposes of their created design. Similarly, the addict is not only misaligned with God-given purpose but also has succumbed to addiction in which the addict's own body becomes a death trap. What was intended to be a blessing has become a curse.

The Holy Spirit offers a direct link to the life of God inside us. *This can turn the power back on to be realigned with God's purpose.* Most drug addicts are familiar with the term *the connection.* It refers to their source to purchase drugs. In the same manner, they will need to make the Holy Spirit their new connection—and He is the Source of life! What a much bigger reward!

Walking into Light: God's System of Transformation

With a connection to the Holy Spirit, one of the immediate changes that occurs is the presence of light. The Word of God refers to God's kingdom as the "kingdom of light," and to Satan's system as the "kingdom of darkness." Darkness is not just the manifestation of bad behaviors; it is a system based on lies with a strategy to dismantle God's power. The behaviors of this system may be evil or they may be hidden behind seemingly "good things." In either case, when people are walking in darkness, they cannot see or comprehend truth. They are blinded by their own heart issues and limited to skewed data their mind is processing in a given moment.

When under the influence, the addict wants to stay hidden to continue using. Since God will disrupt that compulsive need, the addict will push Him away and choose darkness as a lifestyle. This can happen to a Christian as much as to an unbeliever. But when addicts begin seeking and calling on God, they have the opportunity to walk into the light. Because the addict has been in darkness, the light can feel overwhelming. *And that is typically where the fight emerges at its fiercest point.*

The principle of darkness speaks for itself. Darkness cannot be cleaned, removed or swept away. Instead, the removal of darkness occurs only through the entrance of light. The amount of light allowed into a darkened room determines the level of visual clarity. A burning match removes some darkness, but a set of flood lights exposes an area vividly. Therefore, the amount of light allowed will determine the level of freedom that is experienced. It is quite normal for an addict in recovery to have both light and darkness. You might think of this as a room that has some parts lit and some parts darkened.

The Bible says the eye is what determines if light is given access (Matthew 6:22–23). In other words, vision and focus based on God's principles will give access to light. When that vision reverts to a system of survival and coping, the darkness will return. These systems directly compete against each other, and one will eventually outweigh the other. We will look at this again in Chapter 11 when we deal with competing systems of light and darkness within the family system itself.

The Presence of Light

The most important thing to understand about light is that it provides an environment conducive to life, growth and all forms of healing. Just as plants will wither and perish with a lack of light, so addicts in recovery cannot grow and be filled with God's life if they do not remain in the light. But when light is allowed, an environment is established that can make life thrive and grow. Thus, the goal of recovery should be the removal of all darkness.

Darkness ⟵	Person	⟶ Light
Shame, unforgiveness, hiding, sin, covering, brokenness, loss of purpose, loss of identity, unhealthy relationships, unhealthy coping, negative emotions, control, lying, denial.	The level of light = the level of freedom. The level of darkness = the level of bondage.	Grace, love, hope, peace, forgiveness, redemption, wholeness, identity, stabilizing emotions, relationship skills, truth, openness, vulnerability and healthy coping skills.

To better understand the nature of darkness and light, we are going to break down their essential features. In other words, if addicts walk into the light, what does that mean? What happens in the light that causes them to change?

#1. Light Reveals Truth

In Chapters 2–4, we learned how addiction occurs physically, emotionally and spiritually. The body is kept in bondage by the God-created chemical processes being manipulated and turned against themselves. But physical bondage is only the effect. The problems of the addict stem back to the area of faulty thinking, the inability to cope with emotions and the loss of the self-will. The moment that will is conquered by God and the addict steps into the light of His kingdom, a dramatic shifting occurs. In the light, the addict can see the truth of what has been occurring. This is called *coming out of denial* (Step 1).

Truth isn't simply reading the Bible. The Bible provides a handbook for truth, so truth will incorporate that important discipline. But the ability to see truth will include an exposure to the lies that engulfed the addict's thought life and led to emotional pain and eventually the use of medication.

When light comes into the heart, the residue of bondage, shame, sin, unhealthy coping, violation and other issues can be dealt with properly. Like a home sitting in darkness, any dirt, mess or disorganization is revealed when a bright light comes on. That isn't meant to be shame producing. It is meant to offer exposure that can lead to a cleansing process.

The Bible explains that the entrance of light occurs because the Holy Spirit is the Spirit of Truth. One of His jobs is to guide believers into all truth—to give them spiritual eyes to see and the ability to adopt the mind of Christ. This will not happen in a moment. Since the mind has been programmed with many strongholds (lies believed as truth), light will need to continually dispel those areas. Let's see what God's Word says regarding this:

> "And I will ask the Father, and he will give you another Advocate, who will never leave you. He is the Holy Spirit, who leads into all truth." (John 14:16–17)

> "When the Spirit of truth comes, he will guide you into all truth. He will not speak on his own but will tell you what he has heard. He will tell you about the future. He will bring me glory by telling you whatever he receives from me. All that belongs to the Father is mine; this is why I said, 'The Spirit will tell you whatever he receives from me.'" (John 16: 13–15)

In applying this to what we learned in Chapters 2–4, truth is the remedy for the mind where faulty beliefs and thoughts once drove the addict's life. Thus, truth must replace the lies. It must also remain as the guiding force for any transformation to occur. If a point of view other than God's truth is introduced, it will diminish who God is and the power of His promises.

The enemy will try to sabotage the process of recovery by making a lie sound alluring. This is why New Age practices and artificial modalities based on anything other than Jesus Christ will not work. He is the Source of truth! Only truth brings freedom! We have quoted it several times, but this Bible verse lies at the heart of this process: "And you will know the truth, and the truth will set you free" (John 8:32).

#2. Light Gives Us the Proper Vision of the Heart and Character of God

When God's truth is introduced, His character and agenda can be comprehended. After all, it's important to know who He is and what His goals are. This is where all hope can be formed (Step 2). It's not that addicts need to focus primarily on external change—but they first need to know the One who *authors* change. Genuine Christian recovery cannot be imposed onto people in a religious way. A relationship with Jesus Christ must become personal, real and tangible. He must move off the pages of the Bible and into a personal encounter and experience. And that will always happen through the gift of free choice, not by imposing theology.

Addicts must come in touch with God's love, grace, and the understanding of His holy character. They will need to learn to know Him as Father, understanding He has a tender and passionate desire for their wholeness. And because of the intensity of His love, He will seek to protect them from danger. He will use discipline to enforce the importance of obedience.

Addicts' perception of God determines how they see themselves through Him. Thus understanding His heart is imperative. God's nature is composed of His love and His holiness. They are perfectly balanced to formulate the recipe for redemption. God will always have a loving agenda, but it will also be a holy agenda. God's real goal is to make His children holy. He wants to set them aside for His purposes and prepare a generation for His return. While many practical circumstances must be worked out, this is God's central agenda.

People "freak out" that God's holiness sounds like some strict, religious, dreary place to be. *Legalistic* Christianity makes it that way by focusing on performance, to-do lists and various things we must do to supposedly earn a holy status. But in knowing God's heart, we'll discover that holiness is a process of separation. God is holy because He is separate from anything impure. In the same way, He injects holiness into our lives to separate who we are from the sin that has brought corruption. And this doesn't happen through our efforts; it happens by seeking Him, receiving forgiveness and walking in grace. From the place of dependency on Him, He eventually makes us holy. He will align us with His perfect, God-created purpose and identity and deliver us from the sin and brokenness that stole that purpose.

#3. The Light Gives the Proper Perspective on Personal Identity as God's Child

When addicts learn who God is and His rightful agenda, they can embrace their central role in life—learning to be God's child. Living as a child of the King births a brand new identity. It removes the fear and slave mentality that addiction created.

> So you have not received a spirit that makes you fearful slaves. Instead, you received God's Spirit when he adopted you as his own children. Now we call him, "Abba, Father." For his Spirit joins with our spirit to affirm that we are God's children. (Romans 8:15–16)

One of the most beautiful areas of transformation occurs when addicts embrace sonship (or daughterhood) and develop hearts like little children. The Word tells us God seeks after people who will come to Him this way (Matthew 18:3–4).

The identity we each have in Christ is one of the most important principles to embrace. The freedom will come as addicts stand on who God declares them to be rather than on what the past has dictated. Being loved, valued, accepted and honored by the God of the universe as one of His own has more power behind it than words can give justice. It is at the heart of freedom.

#4. Light Allows Cleaning to Occur

As we already mentioned, turning on the light exposes what's dirty or contaminated. This is an extremely important principle to embrace because cleaning must occur for freedom to occur. The light of God automatically has a cleansing effect (1 John 1:7). However, the enemy has worked in the addict's life to strategically plant toxic seeds in the mind. And this is where a deeper form of deliverance must be sought.

Most addicts operate from a system originally created to mask, hide or medicate something that had taken root before they began to use. It could be many things: trauma, death, divorce, physical problems, rejection, abandonment and other events. The seeds planted are not just the actual events *but also the lies attached to them.* These become ingrained in the mind as "truth" (a *stronghold*). Anything that has a *sin root* (personal sin or sin another committed against us) produces shame, guilt, fear and countless other negative effects. The negative emotions sin produces invoke action. The fruit (bad behavior) is simply the life of that seed (lie). Seeing the process in this sense should clarify that all toxic seeds, along with roots and their respective fruit, must be removed (see diagram on page 91). If these seeds are not understood and dug out, they will eventually take root again. All behavior is the actual fruit of a seed. If the focus of recovery is changing behavior without ridding the seed and renewing the mind, that toxic root will spring back up. It may come in the form of another addiction, but it will certainly rise back up.

Therefore, "root digging" is necessary for long-term freedom. New seeds must be planted based on God's truth, and change will happen gradually through the biblical process known as *sanctification* (Romans 12:2).

How Bad Seeds Are Removed

Because seeds can't be seen at surface level, a deeper process must be engaged. For this purpose, it is critical that the addict revisit the past for a season to come to grips with those seeded issues.

We can think of sifting through the past like working through a pile of dirt. The addict must sift through the soil where the seeds were planted to find the ones that are active and producing something negative.

At New Life Spirit Recovery, our counseling process is designed to intensively take the client through all life experiences, especially those related to relationships and trauma. But the event itself does not remain in focus. Just standing as a victim will not bring freedom! Instead, seeing and comprehending the pain of the past has a divine purpose: the seed and the root are exposed. Then the rooted lie and faulty coping that emerged as a result are highlighted. Faulty coping opens the door for all forms of addiction and toxic survival adaptations.

Linda entered into recovery like most addicts, worn down, filled with shame and afraid she could never live a life beyond her addiction. Her current life was so overcome by her addiction, she had piles of rubbish that seemed impossible to sort out. But instead of immediately working on ways to fix her current circumstance, Linda was first asked to write her life story with details about everything that happened in life from childhood to adulthood. To do this in the context of truth, she was asked to allow Jesus to lead the way. Therefore, she didn't depend on her memory alone but asked the Lord to take her hand and reveal what needed to be brought into the light.

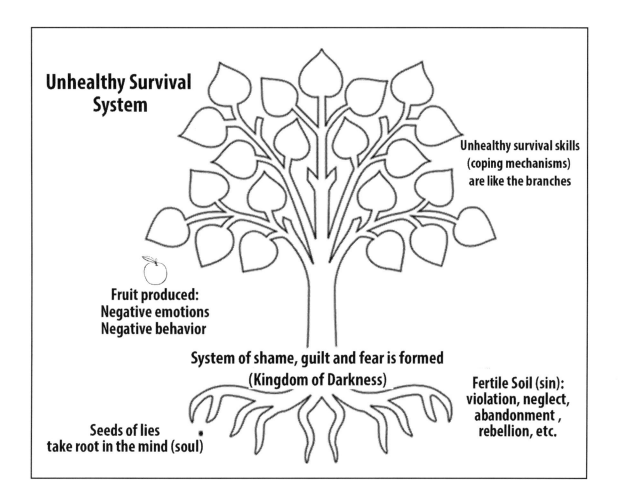

Unhealthy Survival System

Unhealthy survival skills (coping mechanisms) are like the branches

Fruit produced:
Negative emotions
Negative behavior

System of shame, guilt and fear is formed
(Kingdom of Darkness)

Fertile Soil (sin):
violation, neglect, abandonment, rebellion, etc.

Seeds of lies take root in the mind (soul)

Much to Linda's shock, by the time she arrived at her current circumstances, she could clearly see the effects of many other issues she had dealt with. At a young age, a sexual assault had led Linda to check out through false comfort (seed planting). Her violation led her into a severe distortion of her identity, worth and sense of being protected by those she loved (shame, guilt and fear). As her mind focused on these faulty beliefs, her emotions had produced many levels of pain she didn't know how to deal with. Attempting to "feel better," she had used sex and had pursued the acceptance of a man. Her resulting lifestyle of drug use and prostitution all came from a seed, and a system developed to cope.

Linda had run so hard from her inner pain; she had never been able to face that the heart of that young girl had been violated. By being asked to step into that little girl's shoes and feeling what she had felt, Linda was encountering the raw emotional pain that led her to check out in the first place.

That root drive produced all sorts of dysfunctional choices until it was buried by layers and layers of toxic fruit. Untangling the heap of rubbish in her life had to occur before a true solution could happen. A separation of Linda's various life events and choices had to be understood through the scope of God's truth. From there, a spiritual remedy could be applied.

Ridding Sin Damage

Awareness of a problem is the beginning of all change. But it is not enough. Going back through the past is a temporary and purposeful journey. It is meant to permanently extract unhealthy roots to prevent those seeds from reproducing again (See diagram on page 93). Examining the past is not meant to lead to a lifestyle of introspection where the *events* become empowered. Instead, it empowers a *solution*—a method of eradicating the very issues that led to using in the first place.

All transformation comes through the power of redemption and forgiveness. In fact, the central message of the Bible is that Jesus came to give us life. He came to redeem and rescue us from the horrible nature of sin. Jesus is a Cleanser, Healer, Rescuer, Redeemer and Restorer. His job is to meet people in their brokenness and sin. Thus, when He is exposing problems, He is able to stand closely by and pour out His solution.

This occurs two primary ways:
1. Forgiveness must be received for any sin that has been done.
2. Forgiveness of other people's wrongdoings must be administered.

Forgiveness is no "pat" answer. People often say, "Oh, I forgave them a long time ago," when in truth, that sin was just buried. The result was a deep and penetrating root that brought much contamination. Real forgiveness is applying the blood of Jesus Christ directly over that seed and eradicating it altogether. Nothing but the blood of Jesus can do this. To truly forgive others a person must experience a season of going into the "dirt" of those seeded issues to see them in their proper perspective. But learning to access the precious resource of grace— something only accessible by encountering the Jesus who paid the price of that sin personally— is even more important.

God's grace won't say, "Oh, okay, it's over. Let's move on." Grace incorporates a holy standard alongside love. The death and vicious murder of Jesus Christ proves sin is not a small issue. Sin is horrific and horrible. It's an awful human condition. When sin is seen and comprehended in the light of God's truth and love, then repentance has the power to undo sin's damage. That doesn't mean sin won't have other consequences, but repentance can remove the soul's damage and allow us to heal and be whole. Real repentance doesn't diminish sin—it recognizes sin and says, "I see it. I see how bad it is. Oh God, help me. Deliver me from it. I need You! I choose to leave it at the foot of the cross and trust You rather than let it rule me."

Giving and receiving forgiveness can be a process, and it's something that will need to be worked out in each individual. At New Life, we use a variety of tools to facilitate this process because we know we can't get inside a person's heart and do this work for them. Clients in our program not only write a life story, but they also do individual homework assignments on the relationship problems they have encountered through life. Confession, repentance, offering and receiving forgiveness, letter writing, deliverance prayers, renouncing sin and processing emotional issues all are incorporated to create an environment to process and remove those toxic seeds. *Remember, participation by choice is required. This process cannot be forced. Thus, if someone isn't interested in receiving healing, no amount of work or program can bring changes. Only those who are ready and broken and desire to be made whole will see significant results.*

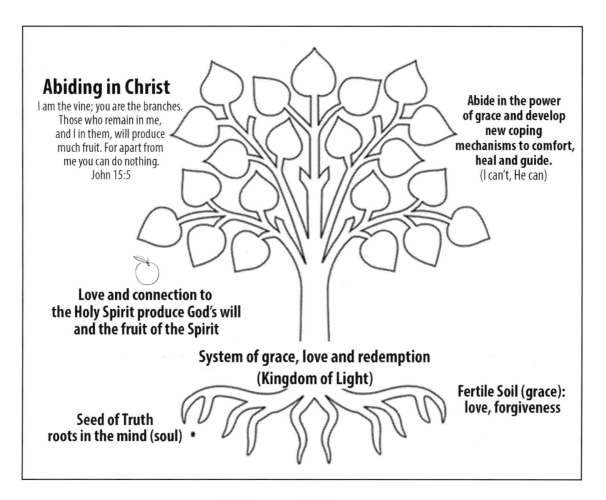

Abiding in Christ
I am the vine; you are the branches.
Those who remain in me,
and I in them, will produce
much fruit. For apart from
me you can do nothing.
John 15:5

Abide in the power
of grace and develop
new coping
mechanisms to comfort,
heal and guide.
(I can't, He can)

**Love and connection to
the Holy Spirit produce God's will
and the fruit of the Spirit**

**System of grace, love and redemption
(Kingdom of Light)**

**Fertile Soil (grace):
love, forgiveness**

**Seed of Truth
roots in the mind (soul)**

The Process of Deliverance

Let's take what we have learned and formulate some specific steps.

- **Bring the sin into the light**—This means the absence of all darkness and forms of denial. Tools can be used for this to occur. As already mentioned, we use a life story and other assessment tools. In the 12-step program this is referred to as Steps 4 and 5.

- **Understand who God is**—This is meant to instigate an environment of hope, not fear. If a person fears God as someone angry, this will be an obstacle that must be dealt with. God is love (Step 2).

- **Confess**—the ability to agree with God that sin is sin. This may be the sin the addict committed against someone or the sin someone committed against them. In either case, confession brings the lie of that sin into agreement with God's truth (Step 5).

- **Give or receive forgiveness**—God hates sin; it's awful. But He loves the sinner. By the power of grace, not effort or merit, we can fully receive forgiveness. The addict in recovery will need to systemically deal with personal sin, as well as gain insight regarding the people in their lives they need to forgive (Steps 8–9).

- **Renounce**—Sin has an influence in the demonic realm. Renouncing sin is closing the doors where that spiritual influence was given access in the first place. It takes back any and all power and footholds that were given to the enemy. Some people require more intensive work in this area when exposed to significant demonic activity. Further resources or additional prayer may be offered.

- **Plant new seeds based on truth** (see diagram on page 93)—Once the soil of the heart is established, the life journey of walking and abiding in Christ can begin. This is the unfolding of God's promises, His purposes, and the establishment of the *life calling*. Therefore, deliverance prepares new soil, which prepares for a new life. But from there, all change will happen through growth of new seeds that root into a new system and eventually turn into new fruit (Steps 11–12).

Stumbling Blocks to Individual Recovery

Some of the most significant stumbling blocks occur in the healing process when the following are present:

- Sin, trauma and tragedy are minimized, and there is no ability to get in touch with the raw nature of pain. A person who goes through the process without any pain has not yet walked out of darkness/denial. *Processing pain is critical.*

- No relationship to Jesus is established; or a true surrender has not yet occurred. If Jesus is not welcomed into the process, the process cannot be done. *He* is the author of redemption, not the human counselor facilitating the process.

- Forgiveness is casually offered without an understanding of the horrible reality of the sin itself. It swipes over the top without allowing the Holy Spirit to cut deep.

- Forgiveness of self is rejected. There may be a stronghold that says, "I don't deserve to be forgiven." This empowers sin while minimizing grace. People will remain in bondage if they don't receive forgiveness. *The blood of Jesus Christ must never be diminished as a remedy for the human heart.*

- Bitterness and resentment create unwillingness to forgive the people who have harmed them. While this is understandably a *process*, a blatant refusal to forgive will allow the contamination of the sin to remain in the addict's life. God will not offer forgiveness to someone unwilling to give it.

> "But if you refuse to forgive others, your Father will not forgive your sins." (Matthew 6:15)

People in recovery who harbor resentments will never be free. Even if sobriety is attained, they will not be able to move into the life God intended. *Resentment is one of the greatest threats to freedom.*

Another way to view this process is to recognize that sin is an actual wound that has been established in the heart. Wounds can be self-imposed or imposed on us by someone else. When a wound goes untreated, it develops an infection. The addict often lives with this reality. Deep resentments can actually cause the sin root to fester and spread rather than be removed. However, when the addict chooses forgiveness, the wound can begin to heal. Forgiving a violator never removes the awful nature of the sin itself. God will never ask anyone to accept sin as okay. Instead, He requires we separate the sin from the sinner and forgive the sinner but give the sin to God. *This is as necessary for family members as it is for the addict. In fact, all redemption and reconciliation rest on this principle.*

Emotional Healing

As we have dealt with seeded issues, it's important to understand that *coping mechanisms* rise out of the rooted issues. *These are typically structures of the flesh that allow for survival apart from God.* We covered some of the manifestations of these briefly in Chapter 6. This is crucial to understand because it is another way the soul gets sick. While sin is always the original problem, these faulty coping mechanisms begin to replace God's solution. Addiction is one of many ways this can occur.

Some Christians think "emotional healing" sounds like a worldly term. But this is not true. Emotions are not evil. They are not wrong in and of themselves. God created emotions to be indicators. Negative emotions have a negative root that leads to negative behavior. Young children begin to learn ways to cope with these negative feelings. When emotions are considered wrong or disallowed in the family system, most children try to stop feeling and thus stop growing emotionally. That's because emotional maturity develops as feelings are felt, then understood at the rational thought level. *But the key is to understand healthy ways of dealing with the feelings.*

As we learned in Chapter 3, when the addict begins to self-medicate, the purpose of emotions is immediately misaligned. Therefore, maturity is impossible. When recovery is initiated, addicts must begin processing feelings at whatever maturity levels they possessed when the faulty comfort was sought. For some addicts, this will be overwhelming. They may have spent their entire life not feeling or using anger or other unhealthy ways of expressing emotional pain.

Transferring from survival mode to God-dependency will provide the remedy. The Holy Spirit plays a significant role in this process. Addicts need to understand what it is like to be held by God. They will need to develop an intimate understanding of their Creator and know that *their* tears are *His* tears, crying *through* them and *for* them. This can be considered a healthy form of grieving. Addicts can discover that He is so involved in their lives, He will actually weep through them and they will experience the pain together. For those with a hardened heart or who lack understanding of an intimate God, this can almost sound like nonsense. But for those who have experienced this in fullness, there is no other more powerful remedy on earth. Grief experienced with God as the Comforter is a cleansing gift. Through it, healing occurs and maturity begins to rewire the addict's faulty coping system. A new coping system can begin to form based on that same comfort received.

God's presence in this process will produce inner peace and joy despite the pain that is experienced. Over time, falling into God's arms will need to become the new method of "getting a fix." Again, this can also be known as *healthy grieving.* Heartache, disappointment and other trials will not end but will now become opportunities for growth. Therefore, the addict needs to be intimately in touch with a relational God who is real, not theologized. This is the job of the Holy Spirit.

> And the Holy Spirit helps us in our weakness. For example, we don't know what God wants us to pray for. But the Holy Spirit prays for us with groanings that cannot be expressed in words. And the Father who knows all hearts knows what the Spirit is saying, for the Spirit pleads for us believers in harmony with

God's own will. And we know that God causes everything to work together for the good of those who love God and are called according to his purpose for them. (Romans 8:26–28)

Where to Go Next?

In the next chapter, we'll see how the addict's recovery can create challenges within the family system. All in all, it must be acknowledged that while radical changes can happen immediately, the long-term goal of learning to love God and love others through Him will take time to develop. If or when the addict ceases to walk in relationship with Jesus, the healing isn't attainable until that connection is established again. As long as connection occurs, growth will happen over time. Addicts will only grow and thrive to the extent they are living in the light and embracing the fullness of who Jesus is.

A Prayer for Long-term Change

Lord God,

I am filled with the hope of Your redemptive plan, both in my life and in the life of _____. So often I minimized Your power because I had a theology that had not yet been realized in my reality. I want to know You and the power You offer. I want _____ to experience that power and learn to walk and live under its influence. We invite you, Holy Spirit, to have Your way. Remove anything that is not of You. Eradicate any seeds the enemy planted and plant new seeds that will produce Your fruit and bring forth a harvest in the kingdom of heaven.

In Jesus' name, amen.

Application:

1. What is your own relationship to Jesus? To the Father? To the Holy Spirit?

_____

_____

_____

_____

_____

_____

_____

2. Do you believe They can transform the addict in your life?

_____

_____

_____

_____

_____

_____

_____

_____

_____

3. Write God a letter explaining to Him your needs, desires and interests in the addict's need for recovery. Tell Him how it affects you. Ask Him to help you understand where you may require a level of the same healing.

CHAPTER 9

Adjusting to Change

Change is one of the most resisted forces in the entire world because even when it is positive, it brings a level of insecurity. Change forces us to venture places we have not yet been. Thus, there is no direct compass to guide us in what to expect. Change also forces us into seasons of adjustment that can be uncomfortable, even painful.

In the addiction-based family system, change will be difficult for everyone. For the addict, change must be enforced as a long-term lifestyle. It will involve resisting the temptation to resort to former methods of coping when the difficulties of life and relationships hit. The addict will need to learn to revolve his life around a whole new reality—the attention, affection and centering of life on God. If an addict doesn't have a Christ-centered recovery, the recovery environment usually becomes the focal point of sobriety. This can provide stability but will never inject the power of transformation.

Addiction was all consuming. Life became centered around how and when to get the next high. Without that fixation, life will need a new sense of purpose, significance and meaning. Addicts fail in their recovery when they can't develop a new centering point through the seasons of transition. This will happen through nurturing a relationship with Jesus Christ and abiding in the inner power of the Holy Spirit.

Not only must addicts face change, but the family system itself will also experience a major adjustment in its formation. Even though the family experienced the negative behaviors and devastation of the addict's lifestyle, the family had in some ways learned to work around this. Since adaptations and survival roles can run deep, sometimes change is painful and resisted. Like a physical body adapting to a faulty homeostasis, the family system may have also adapted to a faulty homeostasis. Members, therefore, may find it more comfortable to remain in the very cycle that promoted the problems.

To see a biblical example of this, consider the children of Israel. They had suffered under the oppressive rule of Pharaoh in Egypt for many years. In that place of bondage, they had lost their will and their individual right to make choices. They had to serve the Pharaoh and be at the mercy of whatever he mandated. When God miraculously delivered the Israelites from slavery, they weren't taken immediately to their Promised Land. Rather, they were thrown into a wilderness season. It was in that in-between state that God required them to leave behind their slave mentality and embrace God's authority.

But when they entered the wilderness, a deeper problem was discovered. They didn't just need to leave Egypt—they needed to walk out their newfound freedom as God's children. And God required trust and obedience to His will and ways above anything else. Circumstances arose that challenged their ability to walk in God-dependency. At times, they wanted to revert to their survival mentality of trying to solve problems and "get by" through their own ideas and logic.

Amazingly, the Israelites sometimes looked back at their place of enslavement as something better than what God had to offer. The change they were asked to go through was difficult enough that they asked to return to slavery in Egypt rather than continue in God's ways. How utterly shocking!

In many ways the addiction-centered family has been in bondage serving the addiction or the person who has been the controlling influence (BCAP). As they responded to the addict's needs and controlling influence, they often lost their ability to make choices. Now even if family members (and the addict) genuinely desire change, there will be points of distress and roadblocks that will prevent them from wanting to continue. They—like Israel—may find it easier to remain in unhealthy roles than transfer to a new system. The first thing to understand is resisting change is a basic and normal human reaction. The next thing to understand is not all change will be behavioral but rather the internal transferring of an authority system. In other words, the centering point will move from something or someone (including the addiction) to God.

In this chapter we will take a deeper look at the transition that takes place when the addict enters recovery. If the addiction was at the center, it was essentially served by everyone. Thus, when it is removed from "authority," the family members must also switch authority systems. If you have not yet experienced this in your own situation, it is still critical to understand these concepts. If at any point the addict relapses, recovery mode ceases and the storm can start anew. Thus, these principles are only relevant when recovery is occurring.

Before we continue, please keep in mind this chapter may be entirely avoided and an unnecessary component of the process if the family already is healthy. However, it's a good idea to be aware of the challenges associated with the addict entering recovery. *Most families will* in some way be able to identify potential areas of conflict during the transition from active addiction to recovery.

Addicts in Recovery

When addicts enter recovery, their families—left to deal with the debris—may have mixed feelings about the recovery. First of all, even when addicts get sober, there will be that inbred fear of relapse. Family members will want to prepare and plan around that possibility, thus maintaining deep defenses. The adapted roles (costumes) everyone has used to survive will not just disappear. Identity and responsibility have been imprinted through these roles, and it can be hard to even know how to separate or exist apart from them.

Preparing for the challenges ahead—if or when the addict enters recovery mode— requires understanding, planning and preparation. By understanding what stumbling blocks and stress points may occur, both the addict and family members can be more understanding of each other's needs. It is also essential to find practical ways to engage in support during this process.

But now, more than anything, the family requires vision. They need to set their aim on the promised land and understand that the enslaving environment must be left behind. Without this vision at the forefront, survival living will stay in place by default. The problem is individuals may have their own vision of what that promised land is meant to be—and it may not necessarily be God's plan. Also, their plans may not even remotely be what the other members desire or need.

To prepare for these challenges, the remaining material will address how to move into a vision, create a plan and work through personal transformation. Since this requires the individual choice of each member, it is not a guarantee.

However, through this season of transition, *it must also be understood that the process of grief needs to be embraced.* Grief was introduced in the last chapter. It involves a way to release the pain of the past and prepare for the changes that lie ahead. It's also the positive way to cope with negative feelings. Grief allows pain to be validated rather than simply bypassed. Without a grief process, that missing or broken place in the heart can become a hole with a vacuum trying to suction other things to fill the void. But through grief, the past can be honored for the positive it contained and released to move into a future that has something more. Healthy grief is orchestrated by the Holy Spirit and involves the ability to cry with Him, release the pain to Him and allow Him to fill us with the comfort of His hope. In fact, the very process of recovery is a season of grief; it is not simply "moving on with life."

There is a time and a place to move on, however. The Israelites had to learn that lesson in a difficult way. Hanging onto their former mind-set had a cost. But we have access to a bigger picture than they did; thus, we have the opportunity to embrace the life that God intended without recycling the pain over and over again.

Application:

1. Do you comprehend the changes that lie ahead require time to grieve?

_____

_____

_____

_____

2. Are you still feeling loss from the storm and thus need time to assess it before jumping into a new "building project"?

_____

_____

Prayer of Grief

Lord,

In the midst of change, I realize some of the things in my heart are a response to a sense of loss. Some of that is loss of my own dreams. Some of it is my own identity. Some of it is the brokenness of this relationship. And some of the loss I can't quite express. But the storm hit, and I have suffered loss. Help me with the challenges that arise in me when I face change. Help me to embrace the feeling of grief as it rises inside me so I can learn how to cope in a healthy way. Help me release the emotional pain that has built inside me instead of living in crisis mode. Help me find a way and place to do this.

In Jesus name, amen.

The Reality of Expectations

There needs to be an understanding of the "in-between" process in seeing the loss of the past and the vision for the future. This is the wilderness season in which one mentality must leave while a new one is being embraced. One of the biggest problems families face in the recovery process is unhealthy expectation on both sides. The addict may expect the family to "snap out of it" and let him or her move on with life—without thoughtful regard for the storm site itself. Addicts can walk back sober into the very home they destroyed and feel so elated by newfound hope that they seem totally out of touch with what just occurred. An addict may even be astonishingly spiritual, focusing on restored faith. This can almost seem insulting.

At the same time family members may expect the addict to be available and make up for lost time. They may actually want the addict to deal with each family member's emotional needs and ask the addict to invest time and energy into those relationships. Furthermore, they might expect perfection overnight without even a shred of immoral or weak character.

What is the actual dilemma? *The vision of what constitutes positive change has not been effectively communicated along with reasonable expectations.*

Mara finally surrendered her life after destroying the people and opportunities around her. Her drug rampage resulted in the loss of her job, children and marriage. Many times her family had tried to assist her, but she wasn't ready to give up drugs, and their efforts were rejected. Finally, they had given up hope.

Then Mara experienced a "Step 1." It was similar to the Prodigal Son's come-to-his-senses moment. Mara saw and comprehended the reality of her addiction and believed there was more to life. She wanted to be changed and redeemed. For Mara, this experience was life changing. It was as if a blinder was released from her eyes and she could see the horrifying truth of her addiction along with the need for help.

Mara launched into her personal transformation process. But in the wake of her addiction were two children, parents and a husband who had long given up hope of ever seeing her function again. Mara, for the first time in over five years, was filled with hope (Step 2) that she could reclaim her life as a mom, wife, daughter and child of God. But her family—so badly shattered by the lies, betrayal and manipulation they had witnessed—were less than enthusiastic. Nor were they hopeful that her recovery program would even work. The family cared deeply about Mara, but she had hurt them so much they were skeptical of any involvement with her. They would be satisfied only by her admission of wrongs and her willingness to serve the family from then on through love and loyalty. She would need to earn back the position she had given up before true reconciliation with her family could occur.

Meanwhile, Mara's own recovery process consumed everything inside her. She had deep brokenness and was processing her life emotionally in a way she had never done before. While following her recovery plan, she was incapable of appeasing her family's expectations. She didn't have the time or the energy for both. As she processed and moved through her personal debris, she had to grieve the things that led her to check out of life and attach to addiction (an abusive upbringing, sexual abuse or other event). She also had to process through the horrible acts she had committed against the people she loved.

Her family wanted to support her but felt their needs should take priority. After all, she had inflicted unthinkable levels of pain and neglect on their lives. Thus, as Mara moved through recovery, she began to feel more and more alienated from her family because they weren't comfortable with her recovery process. The family finally became angered by her recovery and felt the program itself was not helping them but hurting them.

The scenario that offered a solution to this family's problems seemed to make them worse. *What was happening? How could this be? The family was quite simply dealing with the after effects of the storm.* The damage was systemic and had produced a layering effect. The wounds went deep and the healing would require compassion and understanding by everyone involved. In truth, neither side was right nor wrong. Both had a legitimate point of view. Mara was fighting for her life. If she allowed a trigger to set her back into addiction, she could die, go to prison or lose her children permanently. But Mara's family felt cheated. How could she leave after all they had done for her?

If the family had understood the whole recovery process, they would have had healthier expectations. Furthermore, her family needed to understand that even though she contributed to the damage, she couldn't be held responsible for cleaning up the entire scene of the storm. She would be required to own her part, partner with God through the Holy Spirit to be transformed and grow in the power of grace to keep from falling again. She could be sorry for what she had done, but even that would be a process. What she couldn't do was make the family happy or undo the damage. In other words, they would need to take ownership of dealing with the residue inside their own hearts. There wasn't anything Mara could do to change the situation directly other than be truly sorry for her part and begin to reclaim the responsibility she had forsaken.

Healing the family is no small task, but *it is absolutely possible.* In fact, God is a Reconciler and has offered to each of us the ministry of reconciliation (2 Corinthians 5:18). Therefore, He has the right to work in the places that are broken. How He works, however, may be very different from what our human perspective may have in mind. He knows the very depth of each person's heart and offers an individualized remedy for those needs. He isn't as concerned about external changes as He is the inward transformation. Frankly, real change takes time. Like the Israelites, the family will be asked to step forth on a new journey based on God's

FAMILY SYSTEM IN RECOVERY

When recovery enters the system, some systemic changes occur that bring a season of uncomfortable transition. Even though adaptive roles were unhealthy, adjusting to change will prove difficult for everyone

BEHAVIORALLY/CHEMICALLY ADDICTED PERSONALITY (BCAP)

When this role enters into recovery and begins to re-align with Christ, the entire system of control begins to be dismantled. This can be an extremely positive event for the family, but everyone will experience difficulties learning how to understand the nature of that change. If this role doesn't enter recovery, the family can remain under the same system. However, if another member enters into recovery, the balance may shift and the BCAP's role may be disrupted.

CENTERING POINT

PROBLEM ONE

If the BCAP gets well, the problem child will be confronted about behaviors. Boundaries will be enforced that will disallow bad behavior. If in recovery first, the problem one will no longer be blamed for problems, and they may make other members uncomfortable. But the system itself can remain.

GOOD ONE

The good one may feel insecure about the addict's recovery and spiritual journey. They may find themselves uncomfortable with the good behaviors being displayed, and even feel threatened by the changes. When in recovery, the Good One will have different motivations and a new agenda. This may confuse and unsettle the other members.

CHIEF ENABLER

If the BCAP gets recovery, the Chief Enabler will be seriously challenged by the re-centering. Since this role revolved entirely around the problems and deficiencies of the BCAP or other addict, in many ways he or she can feel like an entire job has been removed. If this role gets recovery first, the BCAP and other members will be forced to face their own problems as the enabler's compensation role will end.

COUNSELOR

Without the problems oriented towards the addict, the counselor will feel unsure of a personal role. It may be difficult to adjust around not constantly dealing with a crisis and feeling validated in being the problem-solver. In recovery mode, the counselor will cease fixing and problem solving, which can feel like rejection or lack of love on the part of the other members who had benefitted from that role.

INVISIBLE ONE

If a member of the family enters into recovery, the invisible one may be confronted. Instead of being hidden, the recovery-oriented person may want to encourage and talk with the invisible one instead of denying his or her problem. If the invisible one gets recovery, it can shock and astonish the other members. It could bring the other issues to the light.

authority, not human control. It may be scary, awkward, confusing and strange at first since it can be a lifestyle no one has yet experienced. However, through vision the family can work toward a goal of their own promised land. In the meantime, it should be expected that the family will enter a season of being totally outside the bounds of their comfort. And that's why faith is such an important necessity. In fact, *vision and hope* can be accessed only through the gift of faith—these are the strongest forces needed to persevere through tough seasons of change. Faith allows hope to live and vision to be attainable even when it cannot yet be seen. Thus, through faith perseverance can occur.

> Faith is the confidence that what we hope for will actually happen; it gives us assurance about things we cannot see. (Hebrews 11:1)

If you feel as though this task is overwhelming, it's okay to admit that. However, remember and stand encouraged that God provides the actual resources to make it happen. He says if you have but a tiny mustard seed of faith, you can say to a mountain "*move!*" Not because you can but because *God can.*

Application:
1. What vision do you have for your family?

_____

_____

_____

_____

2. Do you think it aligns with God's vision?

_____

_____

_____

_____

3. Explain your level of faith right now. Do you believe God can fulfill that vision? Why or why not?

_____

_____

_____

_____

A Prayer to Receive Faith and Hope
Father,
In this season of change, I feel there is insecurity. I know what has happened in unhealthy ways needs to be released to You, and that You want to form a new system for my family and me. Even though I want this, I'm afraid of what it may mean. Please inject faith into my heart.

Give me Your vision for my family. Help me see what You want, and let me experience hope that You have a plan and purpose for us. I do not want to get lost in the wilderness. I do not want to go back and live under bondage. Free me and align each of us into Your image.
In Jesus' name, amen.

Resisting Change

One of the clearest signs of an unhealthy family system is its response to a member who is getting well. If the family is healthy and walking in a Christ-centered manner, recovery by the addict (or the member) will be embraced. There will be dancing and celebration for the return of a lost child who was found. We see this example in the story of the prodigal son. The father received the son back with celebration and honor. That was an indication that his heart was positioned for redemption and reconciliation.

However, if the family develops an unhealthy homeostasis to survive the storm of addiction, the addict's recovery will actually disrupt this system—disturbing everyone's "normal." Since human nature resists change, even the addict's *healthy* choices may be rejected.

To clarify this, we will refer back to the survival roles listed in Chapter 6 (see Family Roles after Recovery chart on page 104). This reveals challenges that may occur when each survival role is disrupted by changes to the family system. Please note: Any family member's entrance into recovery will at some level lead to a systemic change in the family itself because all roles are connected. While these changes may be positive for the person under their influence, they can have unusually challenging results.

Balance Shift

While many scenarios can occur, let's focus primarily on the change that would occur if the BCAP were the person in recovery. After that, we can briefly highlight some other scenarios.

When the family's centering revolved around addiction, all survival modes had a direct connection to it. For example, the Enabler's role was established around the unavailability of the addict. The Counselor's role sensed the difficulty of the situation and tried to care for emotional needs. The Invisible One, knowing everyone was focused on the main problems, hid and withdrew without confrontation. The Good One felt obligated to offset the addict's bad behaviors. And the Problem One bore the weight of blame for wrongs that were occurring. If these roles also contained a dependency based on the addict, a change in the addict would obviously disrupt the family system as well.

A season of transition can initially be confusing and uncomfortable. Pain, anger, hurt, betrayal, offense and unwillingness to view the addict in a different light may emerge. The unhealthy adaptation roles can unconsciously be protected rather than relinquished because the adaptive nature of these roles typically contain a root of shame, guilt, fear and other toxic heart conditions. Even if family members do everything right at a *behavioral* level, they are still *inwardly* reacting to the bad soil the addiction had created.

There is simply no easy remedy for this situation except gaining a deeper understanding of each family member's need for healing and recovery. We will address this in the next chapter. For now, take some time review your own role and see how it might be affected by the addict's recovery.

Application:
How you have related to the addict will change if the addict gets better. Explain what might change if the addict no longer needs compensation.

1. Physically (your time, environment, daily routine and anything else on the external level that will change)

_____

_____

_____

_____

2. Emotionally (your inner life—how you feel as a result of the addict's changes)

_____

_____

_____

_____

3. Spiritually (changes in your connection to God and ways you work out your spiritual life as the addict's own spiritual journey begins)

_____

_____

_____

_____

When the Addict Is Not the BCAP

If the person in treatment or recovery is *not* the family's controlling figure— the addiction *not* the primary problem to which everyone responds—a different dynamic can emerge. For example, if the addict is actually the Problem One, the family system must deal with the inability to blame that role for the problems. Yet the system itself will remain just as it did before.

It's common for the Chief Enabler to receive recovery for addiction or codependency *before* the BCAP does. While the controlling figure is still positioned, the lack of enabling will actually remove the unhealthy cycle. This will force the BCAP to either agree with the changes or be unable to function in the position of dictatorship and addictive mentality. Sometimes this will be the breaking point that leads the BCAP into a recovery process. A BCAP without an Enabler is forced to feel the pain of bad choices. However, it will also bring a strain on the other members, thus breaking down the other adaptive styles (see Family System in Recovery chart, page 104).

Roadblocks in the Recovery Process

When the addict returns to a family system that has been wrapped around the addictive dynamics, there can be some unexpected road bumps because of the change in the family's balance system (homeostasis). Let's look:

Roadblock #1. The family system can adjust to addiction where it has been engrained as comfortable and there are benefits to maintaining the survival role.

Adrianna had adjusted around her husband's addiction. For years she had fought to get him right with God. But eventually, Adrianna learned to plan the family around her husband Josh's absence. While Josh was irresponsible in his role, Adrianna held the financial control and was also in the leadership role with the children. A part of her resented Josh's absence and felt hurt and betrayed by his addiction. But another part had learned to hold the controlling role. Even though Josh addiction centered the family as the BCAP, Adrianna played a key role (Enabler). Adrianna's role was, for the most part, more of a mother to Josh than a wife.

When Josh was arrested and faced jail time, he decided to get better. He not only cleaned up from drugs but also experienced inner healing that led him into a relationship with Jesus Christ. In learning his role as a husband and father, Josh was ready to return and be the man God created him to be.

Adrianna, however, resisted this change. Josh's absence had given her a huge responsibility, and if he wanted to resume his position, she was in essence losing her job. They hit a recovery roadblock, not because Josh had gotten sober but because the family had developed a faulty homeostasis. Adrianna wasn't ready or willing to align with the new centering point.

Was the relationship doomed? Could it be changed and brought into a healthy marriage relationship? *It wasn't doomed and could absolutely be made right.* By Josh entering into recovery, the first step was taken. But without Adrianna participating, they would experience what appeared to be separation for a season. The transition may have brought significant levels of strain on the relationship that neither was prepared to face.

This scenario is quite common and is one of the most unexpected roadblocks families will face. The Enabler especially may have adapted so much around the addict's lifestyle that the addict's recovery may cause the Enabler to feel a loss of identity. With so much invested, the Enabler and other members can feel as though they have lost their jobs. In fact, marriages have been known to withstand addiction but dissolve when one person enters into recovery. Learning this and participating in the process of recovery greatly reduces this risk.

Checkpoints:

Understanding your role in the addiction is imperative. If the addict no longer needs your help to survive in the mode of addiction, how will that make you feel? Do you feel rejected or discarded? Are you scared that if you aren't needed, the addict won't have a relationship with you? Are you afraid of losing that person? Do you feel a loss of control?

_____

_____

_____

_____

Roadblock #2. Other Brother symptom will kick in, causing family members to resent the addict's attempt to return home in a joyful way.

As in the story of the prodigal son, family members can feel jaded because the Prodigal engaged in bad behavior while they remained faithful and loyal. These members feel unwilling to celebrate the addict's recovery because they had been working hard and dealing with all the deficiencies the addict's irresponsibility brought on the family system. This is a slightly different dynamic than what we saw with Adrianna. In this case, the family member is filled with very deep resentment and a sense of deserving more than the addict because of a sense of entitlement.

A family member may even be offended that God would grant such a high magnitude of grace and mercy to the addict. Thus, this family member may resort to rehashing an inventory list of wrongs done during the storm of addiction. This condition draws a family's focus to the mess that was created rather than the hope of restoration.

In truth, this reaction is a *serious* heart condition in the family member that desperately needs to be resolved. Its roots can run deep, and it needs as much care as *the addict* so it doesn't yield destructive fruit. It is perfectly fine to feel hurt and need recovery to heal from the deep, painful wounds. But resentment, bitterness and judgment will disallow any healthy family realignment and redemption to occur. It may be hard to accept that Other Brother symptoms are very significant—enough for God to specifically highlight in His Word. The solution won't be for the addict to learn to "eat the dirt of their own sin." Rather, it will come as the wounded, resentful family member learns to receive God's same grace that has been granted to the addict. If this is embraced, the family will be prepared to find healing. Without it, the environment will be toxic to everyone.

Checkpoints:
Am I filled with resentment toward the addict to the point that I am unwilling to celebrate the grace and mercy God wants to grant them? Do I feel I deserve to be honored for what I did in the addiction cycle? How am I dealing with this feeling? Am I willing to get help for any wrongful condition of my heart?

_____

_____

_____

_____

Roadblock #3. Family members who believe the addict should re-enter the family in a way that aligns with their own needs will impose difficult and even impossible expectations on the addict.

It must be understood that family members have been genuinely wounded, and God cares immensely about this reality (we'll address this in the next chapter). However, those wounds, just like physical wounds, must be treated appropriately. One of the roughest dynamics faced by addicts in recovery is the expectations imposed on them as they seek to re-enter the family system,

Addiction wasn't an "all-of-a-sudden-it-just-happened" event. It has a rooted set of issues attached to it. But while early recovery can bring substantial changes, long-term maturity will be needed by the addict. Typically, the addict is emotionally immature and still unable to recognize and deal appropriately with feelings. Thus, when strong emotions are stimulated, there may be problematic responses. Through the different difficulties the family faces along life's journey, the addict will be learning how to interact and engage with the Holy Spirit to make decisions, deal with feelings and mature in other ways. They will also be learning to rely on and be strengthened by God in situations involving spiritual maturity. If the addict doesn't embrace this, relapse is always a possibility.

Family members must understand maturity occurs when the addict learns the benefits and consequences of following God versus relying on false comforters. If members don't understand, they can contribute to a toxic recovery environment. Expecting the addict to change overnight is like asking a small child to drive a car. That is not meant to disrespect addicts or diminish them to a childlike status. The addict may be significantly stunted emotionally depending on when the use began. Maturity will take time to develop. Making decisions to obey God will help the addict establish faith and growth in understanding God's power. While some people may experience a "zap," that certainly isn't the norm. It's unfair to ask the addict to instantly be what family members perceive as a healthy recovery.

At the same time, guidance can be provided that allows family members to discern certain behaviors that can prompt warning signs. The addict does not have a license to be disrespectful, completely unavailable, unloving or overly protective. True growth in Jesus should eventually bring forth the fruit of love.

Checkpoints:
What are my expectations about my family member's recovery? Do I have my own agenda and ideas on how they should respond?

_____

_____

_____

_____

Roadblock #4. The addict will remain unavailable to the family because of a focus on recovery, and the family will begin to fight recovery rather than support it.

It will seem unfair to family members when the addict remains quite unavailable in the first stages of recovery because recovery becomes a lifeline. Without it, the addict stands a very good chance of relapse. At the same time, the family members' hurts need to be understood. This is part of their own recovery: to grieve the loss and betrayal of the past, learn a new way to interact and prepare for the future. If family members can *embrace their own recovery process*, many of these challenges can be bypassed and the process of healing accelerated.

Checkpoints:
Do you feel betrayed by the addict's unavailability? How might you learn to be more understanding? How can you address your own pain of abandonment?

_____

Roadblock #5. The addict claims sobriety and recovery but isn't showing evidence of heartfelt change.

This dynamic can be very difficult to deal with when the presence of addiction has been removed but toxic attitudes seem to remain. There are so many possibilities as to why this may happen, it's impossible to list them all. Sometimes addicts distance themselves from family members because the wounds have been made raw. The addict can't handle the conflict and may adapt a very distant, detached and seemingly unloving response to family. What appears to be resistance may actually be a form of protection. This isn't necessarily a healthy approach, but when someone has damaged emotions and is hurting, it is a common way of interacting with family members.

Other times, family members simply think the addict should respond a certain way. Thus, they may be claiming something is wrong with the addict when the problem is actually with their own hearts.

Finally, the addict may be what's called a "dry drunk" or "white knuckling." This means sobriety brought no inner healing and there has been no transfer to a different control system. This means the addict continues to serve self even if the drug isn't being consumed. This can be an alarming and difficult scenario that requires a deeper understanding of boundaries. Although some continue to live this way, usually, the addict will resume using in only a matter of time. An addict who gets sober but doesn't experience freedom may continue to be a difficult, intolerable person with the ongoing tendency to manipulate and use people for personal gain. Family members may even feel this person was easier to handle under the influence than sober. *Remember, this is first and foremost a spiritual issue that requires a spiritual solution. This issue will be discussed in Family Planning* (Chapter 12).

Roadblock #6. The addict may be asked to deny another member's addiction.

Many times the addict in recovery is not the only family member with an addictive influence. As you recall, addiction can have many forms. And many of the addictive tendencies are generational. Thus, when a child in a family receives recovery, it's possible other siblings or a parent is also struggling with addiction. This poses some unique challenges. While the addict wants to be out of denial and assume a substance-free lifestyle, the family may continue to hide, deny or operate in the storm of another addiction. When this occurs, the family will not be out of storm mode. Thus, the addict's recovery process must be done completely outside the context of that system. The addict in recovery will need to rely heavily on outside resources and have strict boundaries in place for family involvement. This can put added pressure on the system because the family will feel a sense of rejection and betrayal.

When this occurs, the addict will need to focus on their own recovery but learn to intercede and operate from a pure heart. They will need to keep clean from the toxic influence physically, emotionally and spiritually.

Checkpoints:
Is there another addiction with me, or anyone else in the family system, that has not been properly addressed (this may include people, sex, pornography, food, or even using religion in a compulsive manner)? Am I willing to face this for the sake of the long-term benefit of the entire family system? Why or why not?

_____

_____

_____

_____

Supporting Addicts in Recovery

Making the shift from addiction to recovery will require specific resources. Families will be unable to make this transition on their own. While they want the addict to be more functional, they will bear a difficult weight because the addict will be concentrating on his or her own program. If the addict loses focus, a relapse is almost inevitable. Thus, if the families begin to discourage recovery, they will be aiding rather than preventing relapse. To help us better understand how to support the season of transition, let's look at some of the more important ways to support both sides of addiction.

Addicts in recovery will need some specific areas of support:

Addicts need a *sponsor* or *mentor* to walk them through their sobriety. This person will be the main contact for the addict's issues and challenges relating to sobriety. They will also work together to formulate a healthy recovery plan. An addict is prone to isolation and will have a bent toward returning to the addictive lifestyle. A sponsor is someone who has already been on this path and thus can assist in the journey. In family planning, it is a fair request to require the addict to be accountable to a sponsor or mentor—especially in the initial year of recovery when the vulnerability to use again is intense. However, the addict must have the freedom to choose a sponsor. A family member attempting to control this would not be helpful but would be operating from control. Ideally, the sponsor would be Christian and understand the deeper journey of being God's child, not just an addict in recovery. They should also have already attained freedom and have a living testimony of their own. *It is strongly suggested that a sponsor be of the same gender.*

Addicts need a recovery group that will hold them accountable. This group may be a more general AA or NA group that allows them to use Jesus Christ as a Higher Power. Celebrate Recovery (CR) is an excellent option for long-term recovery because it incorporates the twelve steps through a Christian perspective. Often the sponsor will be found within this same meeting. It is imperative this group be apart from the family and be a place where addicts will gain support for their emotional and spiritual challenges. This group is not intended to replace the family, and the goal of family reconciliation should remain. A recovery program must consume a level of the addict's time and energy for the long haul to support sobriety. This will need to be accepted and honored by the family members. Remember, isolation is extremely toxic for the addict. This environment should be a lifeline.

Addicts need a place to live that is free from drugs and alcohol. Sometimes multiple addictions occur, and the housing environment might become unsafe. An agreement and understanding of those needs should be discussed in the family planning. Some family members may have occasional wine, beer and other drinks. This may be something the addict will have to live with. On the other hand, it may be too much pressure to bear initially. Some addicts have to reside in *sober living homes* outside of the house when they're not strong enough to handle the temptations of home and society. There should be an understanding of these triggers.

Addicts need a strong church community that will accept them as they are but lead them into a greater understanding of who God is and the changes He wants to implement. Connecting in a church community is about learning to be a member in the body. If the family can remain in or join a spiritual community together, this will be a place where the family roles can be emphasized and honored. It can be the "together" part of the journey of recovery. Finding a church that supports recovery and is prepared for the variety of needs that are exposed is important. Finding a church environment where families don't feel they need to hide or be ashamed is also important.

It may be alarming to some family members to see how spiritual the addict in recovery gets in such a short time. This may even be intimidating. But in truth, spiritual maturity will take time, and church is an added lifeline for the addict. Allowing the church to be involved is an important part of recovery even though it may be a radical change for the family. Prayerfully, church can bring the family together.

Addicts need the opportunity to gain back trust and to be held responsible. Perhaps one of the toughest dynamics families face is in trusting the addict. This certainly is understandable. Trust needs to be earned. But when the family roles have thrown the balance away from the addict, allowing the addict to regain their position will pose problems. Still, to grow, mature and learn how to live a life of Christ-centered sobriety, this will need to occur. This may include the roles of parenting, leadership, assigning responsibility and other tasks. If this is resisted because of past behaviors, it indicates the family system doesn't feel secure making this change. This is understandable and may take time to restructure. But the long-term goal should be to allow addicts to play out their God-given purpose and role. In others words, the costume of addiction comes off, and the authentic person underneath has the opportunity to thrive.

Addicts need to set goals and follow structure and routines. An addict in recovery will need a plan on a daily, weekly, monthly and even yearly basis. This planning and structure will help create a new system and accountability to a new routine minus the addictive agents. Establishing this new routine may be difficult and often requires assistance. It is tempting for family members to believe they should establish this routine *for* the addict. But in truth, addicts must implement it with the help of their recovery support system (including a sponsor, mentor or other person). As we'll learn later, the family will need to learn a way to love and relate with one another outside the dynamic of control. Thus, the addict must learn to make choices and to experience the benefits or consequences of them. If the Enabler or other members continue to "parent" the addict in an unhealthy way, the former system that brought addiction into it in the first place is maintained. The addict will resist this control and may resort back to what had been comfortable (including using again).

Addicts need to be willing to provide proof of sobriety when questioned. It must be understood, however, that daily questioning, debating and accusing an addict in recovery is absolutely toxic. It will *not* benefit their recovery if you are watching over them and expecting them to relapse. This can actually *promote* a relapse instead of discouraging it. At the same time, family members should research the drug that has been used and understand signs and symptoms of relapse. If the addict is showing a clear display of physical symptoms, it should be agreed upon that drug testing be allowed. This is a delicate issue, and that drug testing may require an outside location such as a drug and alcohol treatment facility or a doctor's office. This is an area that must be covered in the family plan itself. We will discuss this in detail in Chapter 12.

Addicts need to know that drugs and alcohol will not be an option in their family relationships. If family members don't make it clear that consequences will be imposed, the addict—if influenced by a trigger—may have less incentive to remain sober. One of the tools against relapse is for the addict to understand *in a moment of temptation* what the choice to use again will involve. At New Life, we suggest that clients place a picture of their family on the steering wheel or where they will clearly see it everyday to remind them that the relationship may be lost if they choose the addiction. That is not meant to be used to shame the client, but rather to help them remember the cost of that choice. That picture—in the moment of temptation—might save their life. Of course, this isn't always the case, and relapse can happen regardless. But a strong family plan with boundaries helps assist the addict in being accountable.

Families in Recovery

While the addict has some unusual challenges in the early stages of recovery, family members will experience their own challenges as well. Family members must come to terms with their own dynamics in the addiction cycle and then be willing to work through their own injuries it created. This will require a few key ingredients:

Family members need to be in a recovery community around other people who are experiencing similar dynamics. Al-Anon and Celebrate Recovery are examples of places that family members can receive support. When family members have been living in storm conditions, it is important for them to see what recovery even *looks* like. They will also need to hear and understand what others are going through in order to gain more clarity. This is vital for all family members. Children may also need the help of a *child* recovery support group (many CR groups offer this) or the assistance of an understanding adult, teacher, pastor or counselor. Talking about the feelings and pain they experienced is vital for all involved. For children it can also prevent the addiction cycle in their own lives.

Adult family members must be willing to address their own rooted issues to ensure they are seeing through God's filter of truth and not a skewed perspective. While this is important, it does involve a choice. No one can force anyone to deal with rooted issues. There will need to be a willingness and desire to work through an actual recovery program.

Family members must learn the importance of choice, identity and freedom. Anyone who has succumbed to the storm site of addiction has not only experienced emotional wounds but also has often lost their God-given ability to make healthy choices. In addition to that, some family members have lost their entire identity in the family system itself or to the addict under the influence. Thus, they don't know who they are, how to make choices or how to feel apart from that system. This reality reflects the deep need for recovery or counseling. It is identified in Chapter 10 as *codependence*.

Family members need to feel supported. It may seem unfair that while the family needs to support the addict in recovery, the addict may not be equipped to support the family's needs. This is why separate recovery plans are vital initially. It's also why a journey into understanding God's love, kindness and concern is so important. We will pick up in this exact place in the next chapter. For now, let's pray and invite God into that journey.

Father God,
I don't understand the nature of transition yet, or why or how it will turn out. I don't understand entirely my own part or why or if I need to be involved. I don't want to get stuck just because of fear, pride or shame. I don't want to lose out on Your best for my life just because I grew accustomed to the problems of the addict in my life. I want everything You have for me! I want the same attention and kindness You offer to the addict. I need to know Your love personally and to walk feeling supported and validated by You! Please send people who will understand me and support me without making me feel shame for what has happened.
In Jesus' name, amen.

Action Steps:

1. What can you do right now to find a healthy support system?

_____
_____
_____
_____

2. Are you afraid or embarrassed to reach out for help? Why or why not?

_____
_____
_____
_____

3. Do you believe you deserve to be happy? Why or why not?

_____
_____
_____
_____

CHAPTER 10

───────────⟡───────────

Freedom From Survival

Recovery is an individual choice. No one can force a process onto another person unless that person is genuinely interested and ready for change. This chapter is being written for family members who are ready and willing to learn more about their own need for recovery. This is not intended to offend or label. Rather, it's meant to aid in putting clarity and understanding to something often overlooked or misunderstood. Furthermore, it's meant to offer *hope.*

It must be understood at this point that family members are not the forgotten faces behind the main character's disease. God deeply cares and is tremendously concerned about their unique needs. Even though the focus of recovery appears centered around the addict, in God's point of view, each person is precious and needs specific resources and individualized care.

However, it is a well-known fact that family members caught in the addiction role often have a difficult time switching to a role of *being* helped. This can feel uncomfortable and awkward as the entire focus had been on the *addict's* problems. Sometimes family members can be so out of touch from the survival roles of storm living, they are simply unresponsive to the notion of personal healing. Thus, when resources are offered, they are unwilling or not interested in receiving.

No matter where you are, recovery is not about accepting blame or being considered part of a problem. Rather, it is the opportunity to seek freedom *from* the problem.

There are many tragedies related to the addiction cycle. For family members, being bound to the insanity of a loved one's addiction can foster a sense of powerlessness and despair. However, this process will teach that family members can attain true peace and joy despite the addict's choices. Without this hope, the focus of redemption would remain on the addict. But in reality, redemption occurs despite the addict. Thus, it's something that no one can steal.

God's love is the most powerful force in all the earth, and nothing, not even addiction, will separate us from it if only we can learn to *receive*.

With that being said, often family members truly don't know *how* to receive and live in the authentic nature of God's love. A relationship with Him can be sterile, distant or viewed as something that must be earned. That's not because God is inaccessible but because defective filters have made them see Him in a faulty manner. As with addicts, there are roots and reasons behind everything. In this chapter, we will delve into some of these areas in a deeper way.

The History of Family Recovery

The term *codependence* (or *codependency*) was established in the 1970s to describe the family members of an alcoholic. It was discovered that just as alcoholics had distinct characteristics and symptoms, family members also shared toxic similarities (in this book, we put alcoholics and addicts in the same category). The family members had learned to compensate for the alcoholic through ultra-responsible behaviors and efforts to manage the alcoholic's needs. But in the process, the family became unable to perceive their *own* needs. Their sense of purpose and need for affirmation was so centered on the addict that they had adopted a lifestyle of trying to change the addict in a compulsive, sometimes addictive, manner. This system of trying to compensate for deficiencies in the addict-based home became its own vicious cycle.

Although codependence is perhaps most evident in the addict-based family system, it extends far beyond that environment. The adaptive roles of the Chief Enabler, Counselor and Good One will apply to this dynamic. In truth, all human beings are in some way codependent because codependency's very essence is to be dependent on something or someone *external* to fill the needs *within*. Since this need can be met only by God, codependence unknowingly tries to substitute a person or thing for Him.

The cure for codependence isn't simply to detach from people or unhealthy dependencies. And it certainly isn't merely to remove the addict. Rather, it's to gain access to God's resources and allow Him to place relationships in their proper order. While addiction has a ravaging effect, codependence can be just as destructive. Unlimited pain and corruption can occur when the will is subjected to anyone or anything but the Holy Spirit. The person under codependency's bondage tends to recycle this mentality repeatedly. That's why children and spouses of addicts often keep bringing those types of relationships into their lives.

Defining Codependence

In a more practical way, codependence is a set of adaptive behaviors and coping mechanisms used to deal with a family or relationship that is imbalanced. It is bred in an environment where basic needs are lacking, such as love, security and acceptance. At its basic level, codependence emerges to meet these needs by attempting to rescue, change, fix and manage the problems of others. Through caregiving, the codependent sets forth on a mission to nurture the needs of others, hoping their own inner needs will be satisfied. But because the people at the focal point are unable to give—because of their own unavailability—this rarely, if ever, occurs. Thus, the purpose of relationships becomes distorted. Codependents learn to do all the giving, receiving little or nothing in return.

Some codependents become controlling, angry and bitter at the people they want to change. They place demands on them by using tactics of guilt, shame and fear to break down the person they claim to want to rescue. Other codependents are driven by good intentions but are prone to want to please people and bring peace to a troubled environment. Both types learn an unhealthy style of giving in relationships. They also begin to see themselves as catalysts to the needs and desires of everyone around. Unable to have their own needs filled, the codependent believes something or someone *else* holds the key to love and validation.

In more advanced levels of codependence, codependents lose their sense of purpose, identity and decision making ability. They can no longer see themselves as a separate person; they see themselves as an extension of the needs around them. They also become *externally referenced.* This means something or someone on the outside dictates how they think, feel or respond. Like the addict, the codependent enters into bondage. They become enslaved by people. Most codependents feel helpless to change this, believing their own ability to change depends on the people they are attached to changing.

Symptoms of Codependence

Codependence is unlike other addictive behaviors. It takes on characteristics that appear good and right, thus it is far harder to understand. But without authentic help, over time symptoms lead to inner conflict that will disrupt life and relationships at every level. Some of these include the following:

- Being preoccupied with the addict's problems and needs but unable to care for self
- Believing the addict's love and attention will resolve all personal needs
- Feeling responsible for the addict's actions, thus taking ownership of other people's choices
- Attempting to protect the addict or others from bad choices
- Fearing loss of the addict or others to the point of compromise at any cost; willing to give up personal values, morals and beliefs as a result
- Being unable to separate your own emotions from the addict's emotions or behaviors (happy when they are happy, sad when they are sad)
- Trying to please the addict (and others) as the main goal in relationships
- Hiding your own feelings and needs. Feeling personal needs are wrong or shameful, thus portraying needs don't exist
- Being sacrificial as a symbol of love for the addict or others while feeling secretly bitter or hurt
- Feeling abnormal, that there is something defective about self
- Measuring self against others and chronically feeling "too good" or "not good enough"
- Feeling physical exhaustion and burnout
- Experiencing negative symptoms like anxiety, panic, depression and stress
- Believing violation inflicted by the addict or others is deserved, thus unable to stand against their wrongdoings
- Having outbursts of anger or other uncontrollable emotions, followed by no feelings
- Helping the addict and others but unable to receive help
- Isolating out of fear of people or attaching onto people in a dependent manner
- Unable to find a personal sense of identity, seeing self through the addict

An Example of Codependence

To better understand this dynamic, let's look at Veronica. She not only spent the last fifteen years dealing with her alcoholic husband and all the insanity he had created, but she had also dealt with the same dynamic as a child. She was the "helper" in her family of origin as she witnessed her dad's angry alcoholic rampages. She always thought if she could just be good enough for him, it would make everything work. Veronica's innocent heart had absorbed her daddy's problems and needs. She carried inside her the false belief that she was responsible and could somehow fix him. With every stinging slap to her face and each abusive word, Veronica believed something about her was wrong or unlovable. *If only she tried harder next time, maybe he would love her.*

As she grew into adulthood, Veronica carried this toxic mentality. She was performance-based and very focused on finding success, acceptance and approval. She also positioned herself around people who needed her. This helped her feel validated in these relationships. It also caused her to attach to unhealthy people.

It was natural for Veronica to find an alcoholic husband whom she could care for. There was a strong sense of security in being needed by him. While her husband was not abusive, he was not available to meet her legitimate needs for love, security and acceptance. So in adulthood—once again—was an environment where she did all the giving with little or no receiving.

At first, she couldn't see her own adaptive role had transferred from childhood to adulthood. She became the mother to everyone's needs even if the person was an adult. She did everything in her power to make everyone happy and to try to remove the distraction of the problem. Whether she strived to bring peace and order to the home, constantly lavished the family with gifts or became the "ear" that could be turned when in need, Veronica took a heavy weight upon her shoulders. Unknowingly, her faulty point of view caused her to believe that through her own effort she could make things right. However, this entire system was based on a lie. It was never her responsibility to make the problems right. Through compensation, Veronica emptied herself emotionally, spiritually and physically in the marriage. Despite her best efforts and most noble attempts to please, fix and manage the environment, things only got worse.

By the time her husband entered a treatment program, Veronica was numb. It was almost as if she couldn't crack through to feel anything. *She had no idea she had a problem* or that she needed to attain freedom as much as her husband. After all, her efforts were good, wholesome and right.

Veronica didn't need to make any external or moral changes. Nor did she need to be chastised for her part. But she desperately needed to understand a faulty system had been created in her life. She required her own unique healing process. She needed help sifting through her past (see Chapter 8) to get rid of the lies that had developed into strongholds. That precious little girl—lost to a lifestyle of being responsible for problems while being unloved and unappreciated—needed to be reclaimed.

Through the gift of recovery, Veronica could learn the love of her true Father. She could begin to understand her family of origin's dynamics and seek to separate those behaviors from God's agenda. She would need to offer forgiveness to those who had hurt her and receive forgiveness for her own wrongdoing (as described in Chapter 8). Veronica also needed to release her pain through healthy grief, releasing those feelings instead of stuffing them inside.

In doing so, Veronica was rescued from the deceitful, adaptive role of codependence. She learned that Veronica was loved, precious and had an identity based on who she was in Christ. She could serve and love people but not to get something from them to satisfy her own brokenness. Instead, she could love from a heart that had been redeemed.

Who Needs Help?

Anyone in a family system who has been on the other side of someone's addiction will typically develop a codependent root. In fact, over 50 percent of clients at New Life Spirit Recovery carry a primary codependent root. This means before addiction took on its own cycle, the addict had been in the role of caring for someone else's problems. It's imperative this side of a substance program be addressed. If it isn't, the recovered addict is prone to move into problems with the codependence.

It should be understood that it *isn't wrong* to be concerned with others people's needs. But when those needs become so overwhelming that self-care is neglected, codependence has formed and there is a desperate need for help. Furthermore, when another person becomes the guiding influence of a person's choices, bondage is rooted in the relationship.

In the addict-based family system, anyone trying to bring "good" things into a broken system, trying to make it better, will benefit immensely through codependence recovery. While the term and label are things people often fear, ironically *the recovery process won't trap a person into its identity but will rescue a person from its presence.*

Dealing with Rooted Issues

When codependence has seized a person's relationship style, it's easy to think merely changing the behavior will fix the problem. However, just as the chemical substance wasn't the actual problem but a symptom, so codependence must also be dealt with at the root level. The process described in Chapter 8 applies to *everyone* involved. Therefore, that chapter can be used to help codependents deal with their own rooted issues.

However, there is a major difference in approaching codependence from the behavioral, emotional and spiritual aspects. Most of all, the mind-set of a codependent is quite different from a core addict. Therefore, one of the best ways to understand recovery is to uncover these toxic spiritual and emotional issues using God's truth in a loving, grace-based manner. For an in-depth process, we recommend reading *The Christian Codependence Recovery Workbook: From Surviving to Significance* by Stephanie Tucker.

For right now, let's take a look of some of the most important components.

Removing Shame

Codependents have a shame-based mentality that will place a toxic filter on how they see others and themselves. This typically revolves around a system that tries to measure self by a set of rigid moral or behavioral standards. When the codependent feels able to attain a standard, there can be a prideful mentality that says, "See? I'm so much better than you."

This often happens in the addict relationship. The codependent will measure their morality against the addict's and always win. But in almost the same breath, the codependent will look inwardly at the same relationship and feel unworthy, unlovable and not good enough. Therefore, there is a perpetual battle of being too good" in some regards, yet not good enough in others. Unfortunately, this battle can't be won unless there is an understanding of the root of shame.

A shame-based mentality is actually a toxic internal message that leaves the person in a state of self-rejection. The shame-based person may externally grow in perfectionism, people pleasing and performance behaviors. But these are reactions to the dark residue that has trapped them into believing they aren't good enough. Therefore, even though external morality may be obtained, internal bondage is almost certain.

Being able to recognize and face shame is essential and will in fact become the key to the codependent's eventual freedom. Shame has a remedy and requires processing through the events and relationship issues leading to its formation. When shame encounters grace, it will begin to be forced away because the grace of God is based on personal acceptance through the gift of love, not because of personal effort. Therefore, genuine recovery must be encountered with a full understanding of the cross.

Seizing Love

Codependence revolves around a deep misunderstanding of love. Love has become based on performance, people pleasing and the toxic attempt to earn love and acceptance. Therefore, love becomes something that is strived for. One of the most radical and life-changing experiences a codependent will have is the encounter with genuine love. Although we have often not yet experienced it as a reality, as Christians, we have access to this kind of love. Real love is derived from the Holy Spirit. It is not based on human effort, and we can never do anything to earn it. The love of God is a fiery, compassionate, affectionate and holy interest in us simply because we are the object of His eye. We are the result of an idea He formed in His own heart before we even came into the world. No human love system can ever be aligned properly until this love encounter with God is understood. It is actually the remedy but can involve a process at times. Leaving codependent love is not enough. It must be replaced by God's love. Anything else will be simply another imposter.

Overcoming Resentment

Many codependents experience a deep sense of violation and disrespect. As a result, a root of anger forms that can eventually lead to deep resentment. Anger is a secondary emotion akin to a coping mechanism. When hurt, betrayal or other heart injuries are triggered, anger rushes in to protect against the sense of loss or inability to attain a legitimate need. Anger produces a sense of power to express those needs or rise against the attempt to take something away. The self-protective nature of anger has to be validated along with the raw emotion. Telling someone to just stop being angry won't work. "Just stopping" is impossible. A source of pain has brought injury, and anger is the reaction to it.

While anger may be justified, it is not a healthy coping mechanism and can lead to unthinkable levels of bondage and darkness. The Bible affirms we can be angry, but it states if we harbor that anger, the enemy has a foothold (Ephesians 4:26–27). This is typically what occurs with the codependent. Out of anger stems a sense of victimization and resentment. That bitter root will defile many (Hebrews 12:15). In fact, anytime we judge sin, including our own or another's, the power of that sin is measured against us. That's why resentment and bitterness are so very toxic and damaging.

> "Do not judge others, and you will not be judged. For you will be treated as you treat others. The standard you use in judging is the standard by which you will be judged." (Matthew 7:1–2)

Sin always brings an injury, and the only remedy is grace and forgiveness. The freedom God gives to the codependent is not meant to invalidate pain and injury but to give the opportunity to rise above the violations. As described in Chapter 8, a process of forgiveness will need to occur. (This process is dealt with intensively in *The Christian Codependence Recovery Workbook: From Surviving to Significance*.)

Cease Performance

The codependent has adapted to an *external* reference point and typically has grown accustomed to using people or things as the source of truth and guidance. Instead of being able to make healthy decisions based on God's best, codependents tend to take the cues, needs and manipulation of those they want to please. It may seem innocent to want to make people happy, proud or supportive of personal efforts. But the person established with a people-pleasing root cannot live freely; it's a source of bondage. God didn't intend people to have the position of influence over our thoughts, emotions and wills. Rather, He intended *He* would be given that position. Through Him, we can serve, give and love. But when we're trying to gain things from people by getting them to think, feel or act a certain way, we are functioning far from God's heart. Sadly, people can spend their whole life as people pleasers, thinking it's the normal Christian lifestyle and never understanding how radical it is to walk in freedom and the love of the Holy Spirit. True codependence recovery can assist in this amazing transformation process.

Understanding the Roles of Family

In Chapter 6 we covered adaptive roles in the family system used to deal with addiction. *Codependence* defines all roles that try to bring "good" into the darkness of addiction. Through unhealthy adaption, the critical purpose of God-given roles and authority structures are lost. Children learn to function as adults, shouldering adult expectations. Thus, children may learn not to trust or submit to authority figures. Women may bear the burden of responsibility meant for the man's role—taking on the position of leadership and control. While this may be done by necessity, she loses the precious purpose of being a woman with a man's love and provision covering her. She may become so controlling she can't respect authority systems and forces control in many scenarios. The man may leave his leadership post and simply use women to provide for his own needs. He may abandon the family entirely or use work as an excuse to remain detached and unavailable. Or, on the other side, he may take on the woman's role and provide the motherly nurturing his children didn't receive from their mother. If he's not affirmed in his male gender role, he can misunderstand its purpose and naturally function outside this role on a long-term basis. If so, he will never be satisfied or walk in godly confidence in his God-ordained role.

When roles are misaligned, they need to be viewed through God's blueprint. But simply quoting a biblical reference to show the family how to behave is not enough. These are issues of the heart. They require inner healing and transformation that will break the stronghold. The biggest problem arises when one family member reclaims a gender role, but the other members remain in the adaptive version. This is why an individual's recovery can't depend on the other members. Instead, realigning to a proper role happens when God, rather than other human beings, is placed at center.

Claiming Identity

At the heart of codependence is the loss of personal identity. When others become the reference point, personal identity begins to diminish. Eventually *enmeshment* can occur, which is a codependent becoming simply the offshoot of another person. The codependent's identity is also absorbed by the adaptive role itself.

Perhaps the loss of authentic identity is the most dangerous spiritual condition for a child of God. While the addict loses identity through substance addiction, the codependent's loss is far more deceptive. They lose identity by trying to secure acceptance by doing good. This can translate directly into the general belief that God accepts us through good behavior and sees us as not good enough when we fail. *That is a lie!* God loves us because *we are His.* There is nothing we can do to earn that. Our identity in Him is secure. We are who He says we are, and everything else falls under the authority of His truth.

Identity can be restored only by stepping into the authentic identity found as a child of God. Learning to live and be who God created the codependent to be is an amazing journey. It will lead to the life of wholeness, peace, freedom and joy that the Word promises.

Building Boundaries

Boundaries designate property rights and protect against violation and theft by asserting ownership. They essentially say, "I belong to me—and you belong to you." Boundaries signify that if you want to enter someone else's property (physically, emotionally or spiritually), you need to ask permission. Similar to laws that govern a community, boundaries seek to protect what's rightfully ours.

When boundaries function as designed, they allow for an atmosphere of mutual respect. However, when boundaries are neglected, violated or diminished, the lines between "you" and "I" become blurred. Ownership becomes obscure, and personal rights quickly lose definition.

Codependents often lack boundaries because there are much deeper problems happening in the heart. When a sense of personal worth is diminished and identity is lost, boundaries by default will be missing their foundational purpose. The lack of boundaries has many awful consequences. It can mean a multitude of intrusions become accepted as normal.

We will continue to work through boundaries in the next chapter. For now, it's just important to see the codependent's boundary system is often nonexistent or very broken down. Recognizing the need for boundaries is a healthy step toward long-term freedom.

Where to Go Next?

Recovery always starts with a desire and the entrance of light, as described in Chapter 8. Thus, there must be the willingness to say, "Yes, that's me. I recognize the problem." The purpose of this chapter isn't to label you or say that you have a problem. It's always possible that family members have already learned to engage with healthy tools and have worked through these issues. But if there are even some remnants, gaining recovery help is essential.

Next we will address the reconciliation of family members after the storm of addiction. But for now, remember the family system begins to heal by *each individual member* participating in their own recovery process.

Dear Father,

Help me to understand and identify where or how codependence may be affecting me. I dread the thought of a label, but rather than hide from these tendencies, let me face them with the full assurance that You have a better way to cope. Help me understand that You aren't pointing out my wrongs, but rather You want me to walk freely in my proper label as Your precious child. Lead me in paths of peace and wholeness and help me gain everything necessary to walk, live and be free in my relationship with You and others.

In Jesus' name, amen.

Application:

1. Do you recognize codependence in your own life?

   _____
   _____
   _____
   _____

2. Which area is specifically most applicable?

   _____
   _____
   _____
   _____

3. Are you willing and ready to work through those issues? What scares you? What fills you with hope?

   _____
   _____
   _____

CHAPTER 11

Reconciliation

A family that enters recovery together can have new vision, new tools and a new influencing center based on Jesus Christ. It is an opportunity to be rebuilt God's way. The power of redemption is remarkable. When truth, love, honesty and forgiveness are permitted to dominate an environment, relationships can be reestablished as God intended. That doesn't mean it will be perfect or without challenges, but it can be driven by God's principles rather than survival techniques.

What Is Reconciliation?

Reconciliation is the healing that occurs when a relationship that has been strained or separated is brought back together. It removes that wall of separation and replaces it with intimacy and closeness. Jesus Christ came to reconcile—He removed the sin that separated us from Him and gave us access to fellowship and intimacy with Him. Even though He offers us the ability to be in close relationship, our willingness is a critical ingredient. Thus, God's ability to reconcile requires our response.

While many different scenarios may create the walls of separation among family members, the real thing that separates is sin. Where sin and shame exist, family members protect themselves and hide from one another. They drift apart and end up functioning in their own survival modes. Relationships become threatening instead of supportive.

Understanding those issues is necessary before a remedy can be applied. Reconciliation is *not* discounting problems or minimizing their influence. Rather it's confronting them, owning responsibility when necessary and giving or receiving forgiveness for wrongdoings. This is how we are reconciled to God, and it's also how we are reconciled with each other.

Because reconciliation must be *mutual*, many snares can occur. Even if one family member enters into heart transformation, the others may not. When this occurs, reconciliation is not possible at that time because it requires a movement on both sides. Tools of redemption can be used, however, and this journey of recovery *must occur on an individual basis* from here forward.

.   In this chapter, we will look at what reconciliation involves and how it would look in the family system. It is meant to offer hope, direction and an understanding of God's agenda. Most families will begin the journey of reconciliation when two or more members have received individual support and recovery. Thus, it normally doesn't occur immediately. Yet by understanding the purpose, families can learn to embrace the process with hope rather than feel overwhelmed by its enormous task.

A Biblical Example of Rebuilding

A vivid biblical account of rebuilding and restoration is offered to us in the book of Nehemiah. While it refers to the spiritual condition of the nation of Israel, it can absolutely apply to our own families. For many years, Jerusalem had been under the control of oppressive leadership. They had lost their free will as a result—thus couldn't walk in the integrity of their God-given identity. As restoration began, Jerusalem and the temple were brought back under God's control. However, rebuilding was far from over. Despite the end of oppressive leadership, Jerusalem lay in ruins. It was as if the people didn't know how to rebuild and continued to live in a state of survival, disarray and confusion. They didn't understand how to move from one condition to the other.

Nehemiah was a man with a heart for Jerusalem and a belief that God could fix it. Thus, when he learned of the tragic condition of his beloved city, he was deeply moved to action. Nehemiah wasn't going to simply function in the rubble and get comfortable with its abnormal condition. Rather, he was overwhelmed with a holy burden for his city to be made right. Of all the people affected, this one man's burden began the process of a radical transformation.

He began to visualize what God intended for Jerusalem and how far from God's purposes it had become. Yet his focus didn't remain on the rubble. Instead, it shifted to the reality of *who God was.* Let's read:

> "O Lord, God of heaven, the great and awesome God who keeps his covenant of unfailing love with those who love him and obey his commands, listen to my prayer! Look down and see me praying night and day for your people Israel. I confess that we have sinned against you. Yes, even my own family and I have sinned! We have sinned terribly by not obeying the commands, decrees, and regulations that you gave us through your servant Moses.

> "Please remember what you told your servant Moses: 'If you are unfaithful to me, I will scatter you among the nations. But if you return to me and obey my commands and live by them, then even if you are exiled to the ends of the earth, I will bring you back to the place I have chosen for my name to be honored.'

> "The people you rescued by your great power and strong hand are your

servants. O Lord, please hear my prayer! Listen to the prayers of those of us who delight in honoring you. Please grant me success today by making the king favorable to me. Put it into his heart to be kind to me." (Nehemiah 1:5–11)

The plea of Nehemiah was a call to God to take action. He created an environment that made God's response to him irresistible. He didn't emphasize the wrongs exclusively, but he certainly acknowledged the sin and rebellion of God's people. He begged for forgiveness. He asked God to bring reconciliation among his people. As Nehemiah poured out his heart before the Lord, *He focused primarily on the character and promises of God.* Nehemiah turned from the damage of sin and corruption to the nature of God. He believed divine favor was necessary to gain the resources to rebuild. He believed God would come to his assistance.

God's grace was the reward of that transaction; it prompted a full restoration. God forgave the sins of the nation and provided the resources for Nehemiah to rebuild.

Despite God's favor, opposing forces immediately tried to dismantle the project. The Bible says enemies showed up at the scene of destruction and began to mock Nehemiah and discourage the efforts, deeming them "useless." Had Nehemiah allowed the pressure of those attacks to deter him, the walls would have never been restored.

Nehemiah didn't trust in human efforts or plans. He trusted in the God who had given him a promise and who owned all the resources of heaven and earth to assist him. Therefore, Nehemiah's only real threat was leaving God's authority and venturing into an independent mode of survival.

This remarkable story has a happy ending and contains incredible truths that apply to our storm sites. Like Nehemiah, we too must be willing to pray over and honestly assess the damage that was done and how it hurt God, others and ourselves. We need to seek forgiveness. Nehemiah spoke on behalf of his people. We too can enter the throne of grace as intercessors for the needs of everyone. We just can't actually *do* anything to try to change their hearts. Furthermore, we can't force the reconciliation of a relationship. But what we *can do* is use prayer as a weapon of true change. We too can receive the resources and assistance of God Almighty. Above anything, we must believe God wants more for us than to live among the rubble. We must believe His power is above the storm itself.

Using Nehemiah, let's break down the components of what rebuilding required (to put this in the proper perspective, we recommend reading the book of Nehemiah in the Old Testament).

Repentance

Nehemiah approached God with humility based on his own sinful condition. Imagine if he'd blamed his fellow brothers and sisters, asking God to punish them for what they'd done wrong while asking Him to grant Nehemiah personal favor. Had that occurred, restoration of the city itself would never have happened. Nehemiah may have gone on with life but without the reward of total restoration.

Nehemiah's plea wasn't filled with resentment but brokenness and sadness. This cry from his heart was felt and understood by God. Nehemiah was willing to take ownership of the wrongdoing while being willing to tackle the task of rebuilding. He used *God's solution* as His motivation rather than condemnation, shame or guilt toward himself or others.

In our own circumstances, anger is a likely reaction to the violation and sin that have occurred. However, through recovery, we learn that anger is actually an expression of pain. Through healing, God can work through that pain and then give family members a burden to see the family restored. This may not happen right away, and the best possible starting point is individual recovery and restoration.

Meditation Point:

Can you look at your own family and see the damage that has occurred and feel the sadness and grief over what has been? Are you angry? Do you struggle with blaming? Have you been able to walk in the reality of God's forgiveness?

Prayer

The purity of prayer matters to God. It isn't in the words that are spoken but in the attitude of the heart. Nehemiah knew his God. He also knew the sin that had occurred. But in the moment, he understood God was bigger than the damage. He was bold to ask God to bypass circumstances and bring divine provision. Because his heart was in the right place, God honored his prayer.

We are promised in the Word that God will respond to our prayers when they are prayed from a pure spirit.

> "Keep on asking, and you will receive what you ask for. Keep on seeking, and you will find. Keep on knocking, and the door will be opened to you. For everyone who asks, receives. Everyone who seeks, finds. And to everyone who knocks, the door will be opened." (Matthew 7:7–8)

That's why our own process of recovery is so essential; it puts us in a position where our prayers can flood heaven. At the same time, prayers don't rely on us—they rely on grace. Thus, the attitude of the heart must be dependency.

Meditation Point:

Do you feel confident of grace? Are you afraid to ask God for provision? Why? Does the storm feel too overwhelming?

Application:

Spend some time talking with God about this and ask Him to help you. Then you have the option to come boldly to throne of grace and ask for help and divine resources.

So let us come boldly to the throne of our gracious God. There we will receive his mercy, and we will find grace to help us when we need it most. (Hebrews 4:16)

Claim a Promise

Nehemiah demonstrated a powerful tool of redemption. He prayed and made a request to God based on the very promise He had given. He spoke back that promise before the Lord. How could the Lord deny His own Word? The answer is that He couldn't. Based on His faithful nature, God was obligated to fulfill His promise. And He did. Nehemiah was the vessel that allowed God to move forward.

Application:

Find a promise you believe God has given to you or your family and then speak it back to God. Even when you can't see the answer, keep His promise in the forefront and continue to believe what it offers. For example, Jeremiah 29:11 says, "For I know the plans I have for you," says the Lord. "They are plans for good and not for disaster, to give you a future and a hope." This promise can be prayed back to God.

_____
_____
_____
_____

Wait for God's Resources

Nehemiah had to wait for God to produce the resources. When He did, Nehemiah was moved into action. Nehemiah understood he was operating through God's provision. Thus, his confidence was based on what God could do, not what *he* could do. In our own situations, we too must learn to rely on God's provision rather than clinging to our survival mode. We must be more set on God's directing than on our responding to crisis in unhealthy ways. Because this is so difficult at first, support and recovery are crucial.

Meditation Point:

Are you ready to wait for God's provision? Do you struggle with grabbing the control reins and trying to fix it yourself?

_____
_____
_____
_____

Understand Your Role and Allow Other People to Perform Their Own Roles

When Nehemiah got to work on the project, he had to facilitate redemption by allowing each family to take ownership of a gate. Had he been solely responsible for the entire project, it would have never gotten done.

We too will need to claim ownership of our part but resist the temptation to own other people's problems. For family members accustomed to overcompensation, this can challenge us immensely.

Application:
Define your part in cleanup and recovery as you see it right now. Define the addict's part. (We will address this through family planning in a detailed manner.)

_____
_____
_____
_____

Overcome the Challenges

Nehemiah dealt with troubles both externally and internally. The enemies of Israel actually scoffed and mocked Nehemiah. They threw language of discouragement to upset his plans. They tried to speak shame over the rebuilding team and rip away the very promise God had granted them. And if that was not enough, Nehemiah's team began to give up and walk in defeat. Nehemiah had to cling to truth and rely on the reality that God was controlling the situation. If he had lost focus, the project might have failed.

We will face challenges that originated in the demonic realm. The enemy uses people to discourage us and try to defeat God's plans for us. They may be people in our own family systems. That doesn't make them evil, but it can mean there are two competing systems. Because not all family members will necessarily seek recovery at the same time, the family may have varying degrees of darkness and light within the same family system.

The concept of walking in the light was introduced in Chapter 8. It should be emphasized again; the dark isn't necessarily an immoral lifestyle. In fact, darkness and light are referring to two operating systems (See Table 3.1). When these competing systems are at war in one family, there may not be peace in the home initially. In fact, Luke 12:51–53 reminds us that a sort of war can erupt:

> "Do you think I have come to bring peace to the earth? No, I have come to divide people against each other! From now on families will be split apart, three in favor of me, and two against—or two in favor and three against.

> 'Father will be divided against son and son against father; mother against daughter and daughter against mother; and mother-in-law against daughter-in-law and daughter-in-law against mother-in-law.'"

These astonishing words of Jesus don't mean families must remain in this condition, but it does reflect the disruption created by two competing systems. While restoration is always the heart of God, a time of turmoil and separation can occur that is not a direct result of the addiction but of spiritual change. This doesn't mean the person or people living in darkness are evil or bad—it just means they are walking in a form of denial and using coping mechanisms to deal with life outside God's purposes (Chapter 8). They may or may not be Christians. Sometimes Christians walk in varying levels of denial.

It must be understood that darkness hates the light because light *reveals* things that aren't right or clean (John 3:20). But the conflict should be met with love and compassion. When a family member begins to walk out of survival living and into God's light, it isn't a license to use Jesus to control, shame or force change. In fact, doing so reflects the system of darkness. Only genuine love and the empowerment of the Spirit eradicate darkness.

Table 3.1 Darkness versus Light

The System of Darkness	The System of Light
Covers, hides, lacks honesty.	Opens, reveals, sees everything in light of truth.
Human control devises this system.	God's authoritative Word and His Spirit are guidance and reference point. Control is given to Him.
Adaptive roles cover.	All coverings are removed; identity is established in Christ.
Shame motivates, says "not good enough."	Grace covers wrongdoing and sin and says, "You are okay, I'm okay—God's grace is enough."
Refuses to forgive; resents.	Receives and offers forgiveness for sin.
Emotional turmoil.	Begins to experience peace and joy despite circumstances.
Uses unhealthy coping.	Begins to feel, grieve and rely on the power of the Holy Spirit to bring comfort.
Religious activity to look good.	Authentic brokenness; all effort relies on the cross.

The purpose of this book is not to create separation by exposing this dynamic but to overcome darkness by bringing it into the open. This difficult truth causes more breakdowns in the family system following recovery than we can count. Before you feel disappointment or despair, it must be clear that the light consumes the darkness; the darkness cannot consume the light. When light leaves, darkness is the natural result. This means as long as light enters the family system, the whole system may eventually be consumed by it. Its very presence is the flicker of hope even though it may originally be met with resistance.

There may be difficulties in the meantime, but each member who experiences the light will be filled with the peace, power and goodness of the Holy Spirit. They will find the reward to be *Him.* It will give them the ability to persevere and to love with Calvary love—a love that recognizes the human condition as in need of redemption.

When Nehemiah completed the project, it was dedicated unto the Lord. God's Holy City had been reinstated to its purpose and identity. What an awesome celebration! While you are going through the in-between season of this journey of rebuilding, keep the goal in mind. Also, remain steadfast in the belief that the Author of Redemption is the One who is fully capable of bringing the rebuilding project to fruition. Set your heart, affection and attention on Him and Him alone. No matter the opposition, no matter the resistance, no matter the nature of the circumstance, your God IS enough!

A Prayer to Encourage in the Rebuilding

God,

I want to be aligned with You and Your resources for rebuilding. However, when opponents start to attack me, help me see You. Teach me to respond and walk through the process of rebuilding with You holding my hand and guiding me. I know you are stronger and bigger than any of the challenges we have in our family or relationships. I can't fix _____, but I can bring the needs of my family before You. I can declare that I can do all things through Christ! I believe in the promise You have given me. And please confirm a special promise for me so I can cling to it even when I can't see it with my eyes. Fulfill Your own plans for our family! Bring us back to Your created design! We will honor, praise and serve You!

In Jesus' name, amen.

Meditation Point:

Is there anyone in your family who may continue to live in denial? Are you afraid of exposing yourself? Do you still want to hide? Are you ready to live in the light of God's system?

_____

_____

_____

_____

What Does it Look Like to be Christ-Centered?

The task of rebuilding is a very unique journey. It requires a new system to be resurrected in place of the former. It also requires the family's homeostasis to receive a new source of centering.

Even while we wait for God's divine resources, we can visualize the goal of the construction site. God's heart operates so utterly unlike the adaptive mentality of the addiction-based family system! These principles may seem almost unattainable. But ironically, these very conditions can return the family to a normal and healthy homeostasis. Just as we see a physical body in robust health—all parts functioning as designed—we need to see what the healthy family's centering point entails.

But before reviewing these principles, remember this is the *goal* not the *current reality.* Thus, we plead with God as Nehemiah did to begin rebuilding our own "city" into His created design.

Vision for a Christ-Centered Family

A healthy, Christ-centered family has elements that honor God and bring His reality into a sick and broken world. God's will is that His name be honored; thus, He's moved to action as our desires align with His. This family can be the light shining in the darkness and helping the world know God is real. If you are a child of God (which you most likely are if you are reading this book), then it is one of your deepest desires to walk out your family relationships as God intended. But if it doesn't happen immediately or if these plans are somehow shattered, remember this: You can align yourself personally to exist as a member of God's family. Thus, these principles don't require the family's involvement to be real and activated in you. We will now look at some critical areas of reconciliation and a healthy centering on Christ.

The home is centered on and operates through the truth—both in the Word and through the Spirit.

As we have learned, truth is not found in religion but *in authentic relationship.* This ability to walk in truth will affect each person individually and give them the ability to grow and nurture their own relationship with the Lord. It will also create an authentic and vulnerable atmosphere for all family members, giving them permission to expose weaknesses rather than cover them.

The crucial first ingredient for family transformation is to stop concealing, hiding, pretending and walking around problems and start opening, sharing, communicating and speaking feelings. Obviously, if one member is ready and the others aren't, difficulties can emerge. Some vulnerability isn't possible when the other person is unhealthy. That's when finding a healthy and safe recovery group will help. There you have the opportunity to put some of these skills to practice outside the context of your own family system. Remember, the one family member in recovery can inject hope and begin to change the overall dynamic in a positive way.

Laura was a Chief Enabler in recovery. She had poised herself as strong, together and in control from the beginning. But through recovery, that outward role had to be removed. Now Laura began to direct conversations based on truth. She voiced her inability to align with things that opposed her belief systems. Furthermore, she wasn't able to coat everything over. In fact, Laura was processing pain and was seemingly weak instead of strong. This confused and upset the other members.

Truth invaded this home. While the family struggled with her adjustments, Laura began to bring a pure heart into the home. Rather than exploit her sense of righteousness ("I'm good and you're bad"), she lived a life that had been softened through Jesus. Truth didn't just force her to tell everyone what was wrong. Instead, it gave her permission to remove her faulty costume and introduce herself authentically to the world around her. The pain of this was immense as Laura was vulnerable to rejection.

However, over time her weakness became meekness. She became more and more equipped to be strong in the Lord. Though her change in roles at first came with difficulties, the entrance of truth and love eventually broke down the walls of denial and brought everyone to seek help and be healed.

Holy Spirit love is present and its influence is active.

Truth without love is like a clanging cymbal. It will be obnoxious, harsh and without compassion. That's why where there is truth, love must be wrapped tightly around it.

Love has been misinterpreted in many different ways under the influence of addiction. For the Enablers, love may have been compliance and the desire to please the addict. Love may have been lying to appease and protect the problems members were facing. When real love strikes a person, it brings a holy standard alongside it. Love is something very different than it was in the survival role. The love of God is based on His unconditional affection for the human race. He is intentional, kind, caring, compassionate, gentle, gracious and good. Yet He is radically opposed to darkness. Love will not co-sign, allow or align with sin because sin wrecks the human heart. A God who loves will not allow our spiritual or earthly enemies to prey on us with His blessing or approval. He will warn, protect and adamantly do anything He can to rescue us from sin.

In the same manner, authentic love will engage with people as they are—loving them without condition. It will recognize their sinful mentalities as something that will hurt them and everyone else. Therefore, the focus isn't just on self-protection from the person engaged in sinful behaviors but on concern for that person's heart. Like Nehemiah, family members can bear a holy grief for the family member they love.

Truthfully, and sometimes painfully, love isn't based on good conditions. Love will manifest the very most when its presence comes against darkness and sin. This is Calvary love—it loves those in a condition of being unlovable.

It is impossible for the family to immediately switch to this sort of love. It will take time to nurture love and to mature and grow in it. This love isn't human love but *agape love*: the love derived from the Holy Spirit.

Furthermore, we mustn't despair when faced by the requirements of love. In reality, love redeems. It is the most powerful influence on earth. This is what the Word says:

> And I am convinced that nothing can ever separate us from God's love. Neither death nor life, neither angels nor demons, neither our fears for today nor our worries about tomorrow—not even the powers of hell can separate us from God's love. No power in the sky above or in the earth below—indeed, nothing in all creation will ever be able to separate us from the love of God that is revealed in Christ Jesus our Lord. (Romans 8:38–39)

A love like this is unstoppable. If you don't yet house that love, it simply means you have a journey to behold! (The *Christian Codependence Recovery Workbook: From Surviving to Significance* and *A House that Grace Built* walk through these principles step-by-step.) If all family members eventually housed pure love, then intimacy, wholeness and purpose would allow that family to reflect God's design by default. That's why God's core agenda for us is to love Him and one another.

The home operates through freedom.

The operating system of a healthy family is based primarily on the principle of freedom. Each family member's right to think, feel and make choices is considered sacred. Ultimately, it is understood that the objective for everyone is to be aligned with God through the power of the Holy Spirit—not merely managed externally to accommodate the family itself. Thus, family members don't directly try to change other members' thoughts, feelings or choices.

This may lead to difficulties when controlling family figures aren't ready to release that role. If members still try to maintain control (especially if they are in the lead role of the family), it is difficult to learn to be controlled by God yet still honor and respect those roles.

Being controlled by the Spirit is the goal of our own journey of recovery. This control can never be exchanged for a human being's mandates. However, that doesn't mean we can do whatever we want using Jesus' name as justification. It means we must learn to align our thoughts, feelings and choices to the Spirit—and then respond to human control in accordance with that.

In truth, where love exists, submission will follow. Where love exists, control is unnecessary because love responds for the betterment of the others. But since love is pure, it will not submit to sin or to a faulty control base. It will submit to a person to honor them, love them and display that their needs matter.

George desired to maintain control of the home following his son's rehab. But Joshua was no longer willing to be dominated by a system that assaulted and shamed him. However, *God's love in Joshua* recognized that George was experiencing spiritual and emotional conflict and needed God's redemption and love. Therefore, rather than disrespect his father's authority, Joshua learned to respond in loving ways. When his dad said things like "Joshua, you are stupid; you always have been stupid," Joshua learned to respond in love: "I'm sorry you feel that way. I don't see myself like you do."

But Joshua couldn't only defend against unhealthy control; he needed to learn to honor and submit whenever possible. When Joshua had the opportunity, he would inject a meaningful way to express love to his dad and to submit to something his dad requested.

Joshua even moved from the home to honor his need to stop depending on his parents. But he didn't detach. He remained available and involved by choice and not because he needed them to fulfill his own agenda.

Over time, Joshua affected his dad. His dad came to know Jesus and experienced his own freedom as a result. Reconciliation occurred.

While it may not seem attainable, it only takes one heart that has been injected with this powerful love to overcome the forces of darkness in someone else. Love is very, very powerful. That's why the Word says we can't overcome evil with evil but need to overcome it with good (1 Peter 3:9).

The home validates God-ordained roles and responsibilities, encourages members to grow respectively in their individual purposes and lovingly holds people accountable to their roles.

In honoring these roles, compensation can be done out of necessity, but it won't ever obstruct the fundamental purpose and plan of the family through God's heart. Furthermore, people are not defined by their roles—thus their unique and individual identities highlight and accentuate the roles; they don't replace them. In other words, a *mom* is one role in life. It's very important, but underneath that role is a person with unique needs, characteristics, attributes and a God-given identity. So the "mom role" does not entirely define the person.

Healthy roles were addressed briefly in the previous chapter. What's important to understand is that God-ordained roles aren't rule oriented but heart based. Men are called into their roles because God created them for leadership and placed a desire in them to be respected. They will never be satisfied until that role is aligned. Women are created to be honored, loved and provided for, not out of obligation but out of desire. A woman who operates outside that role will never be satisfied until it is fulfilled. The sadness of broken roles may tempt us to point fingers at how people have failed us. But really, these broken roles are an opportunity to allow God to fill in the gaps.

We can be our roles first and foremost before God. He can nurture and develop us and give us satisfaction. But prayerfully, over time, we can realign in our human roles or let God prepare us for future healthy relationships.

Learning to remove the adaptive role and replace it with His authentic identity is an individual journey of healing that cannot be addressed fully in this material. However, it is addressed extensively in our other material. We encourage you to seek additional assistance to learn how to transform from the role of survival into the role of God's identity and significance (see Chapter 10).

The home has a fundamental system of grace where problems, inadequacies and sin have a remedy through forgiveness.

Grace does not willingly allow sin but loves a person beyond their flaws and wrongdoing. A system of grace filters others through the perspective of Jesus—it sees weakness as an opportunity to be made strong in Jesus. Grace also fundamentally knows that Jesus defeated sin and has the remedy to deal with it. Forgiveness is not merited by behavior or duty but through humble dependence on Him.

It can be difficult to create a dynamic of grace where shame is still present because shame will attempt to discredit and break down the power of grace. Shame will focus on what's wrong, inadequate or broken. It will point to wrongdoing and sin and everything that doesn't measure up. When one person is operating by grace and the other by shame, it can seem unfair and difficult to learn how to mingle together.

However, grace is more powerful. It must not fall victim to the tactic of shame. Shame can only try to intimidate the heart by pointing to flaws. But grace has Jesus set upon it to cover those inadequacies and shortcomings. Grace rules as we seize it and walk under its influence by keeping our eyes fixed on Jesus.

The home operates by mutual respect and uses boundaries to designate individual rights and protect the safety of all members involved.

A boundary distinguishes lines of responsibility. Just as a fence between yards draws the property line, so each member has their own distinct life: body, soul and spirit.

Visualize two homes side by side with a fence to designate separation. Each homeowner is responsible for their home's upkeep. By ownership, property rights are awarded. Thus, anyone who enters the other's property must ask permission.

Entering someone else's house without permission, even in the name of "helping," is a boundary violation. Cleaning your neighbor's house may be helpful but not when that task is unauthorized. In truth, it would be deeply disrespectful (and illegal) to barge into someone's house to "help" in this way.

The Enablers of the family tend to have this mentality. The addict may resent the help but then become dependent on and feel entitled to it. This eventually promotes an environment where the addict no longer has to be responsible because someone else is cleaning, cooking and doing their laundry. There is no incentive or natural benefit in taking ownership of this responsibility when it is already being done.

The addict often inflicts more outward violations. In fact, while the family member is cleaning the addict's "house," the addict may jump the fence and steal or destroy their unattended property. The family members feel doubly betrayed. They feel unappreciated for their efforts and violated by the assault of the addict. No wonder there is such turmoil! No one understands or respects personal rights. Everyone feels intruded upon and violated.

All this needs to be untangled. A boundary will clearly identify what is rightfully mine and what is yours. It will affect other areas including responsibility, identity, emotions and behaviors. Through boundary planning, personal property has to be reclaimed. Enablers often extremely neglect their own side of the fence and focus instead on cleaning up someone else's messes. Turning this around will be challenging! But it will ultimately allow everyone to align and find the opportunity to rebuild.

Eventually, through healthy boundaries fences of respect can be established. This system of respect will take time to develop, but it is at the heart of reestablishing a healthy home. "We" had become an enmeshment because boundaries no longer existed. Through recovery, family members must become separate entities physically, emotionally and spiritually while working together in relationship.

Ironically, boundaries do not separate but prepare for true intimacy. True familial love can only occur when members are whole and healthy and can see themselves and others as precious. Thus, while boundaries seem to separate, they actually prepare for the intimacy that allows closeness in an authentic way.

We are called to be one with Jesus—the closest and most intimate relationship possible. Yet Jesus honors our unique individualities. He establishes us as persons and respects our ability to make choices. When a family walks into this level of healing, the sweetest, most beautiful reflection of God's heart can be experienced. (For more information about boundaries as it relates to addiction, please refer to Chapter 7. Our other materials will address boundaries in detail.)

Back to Wholeness

While families may each have their own dreams or ideas of a healthy family system, those ideas and dreams must be surrendered at the feet of Jesus. The journey into alignment may come with all sorts of difficulties. Since we cannot change other people, your biggest job right now is to find freedom, remain free, disconnect from wrongful mentalities and reconnect to

God's system. We can have hope that God can do this in us. However, our hope must never become anchored to another family member's change. It must never focus on the external. It must remain on being satisfied and secure in the presence of God's love. The most important step in this process, therefore, is not to concentrate on how your family member must change, but to stand ready, willing and available as a vessel God can use to carry light and bring freedom.

A Prayer for Healing
Lord Jesus,
I can't move an inch unless I'm dependent on You. I don't want to stay in the survival mentality, but I realize moving into reconciliation may not occur in my own timeframe. Help me resist the urge to bypass my own needs and to focus on my family member. Help me walk with You and embrace the tools You want to offer our family and me. Soften my heart to You so I can listen for Your direction, be comforted by You when I'm hurting and find healthy resources that will lead me into personal transformation. I believe You have good plans for us, plans to prosper us and not to harm us, plans to give us hope and a future. Please make me ready for this and provide supernatural grace to allow You to hold and carry what is broken, missing or invalidated in the in-between season of change.
In Jesus' name, amen.

CHAPTER 12

―――――――――――――― ⟲⊙⟲ ――――――――――――――

Family Planning

At the site of the storm where rubble had lain, new plans form vision, hope and the activity of rebuilding. All building projects begin with a plan. Blueprints allow the structure of the site to be established and all necessary resources to be supplied. These plans must be facilitated by a general contractor who will string together a wide range of resources and levels of expertise. Should multiple crews create multiple versions of the plan, chaos will quickly erupt. One blueprint will overtake another until several versions collide and disrupt any sort of normal building process. In fact, the greatest necessity for any building project is that the builders agree on the finished design and then build step-by-step to attain that goal. Then all the contributors to the project will be working toward that one plan.

The complexities of rebuilding the family system after the storm of addiction are just as intense as a physical construction site. And the first thing needed to move forward is for the family to develop a plan that contains *one set* of blueprints. If multiple family members have varied ideas of what the family recovery plan should be, chaos can break out. What one member deems as an appropriate goal may compete with another member's very different agenda. Thus, it is essential that each family member is able to express needs, develop boundaries and build healthy expectations.

Setting Expectations

Planning sets the course for healthy expectations. Imagine if you expected a general contractor to build a three-bedroom ranch home, and instead he built a ten-bedroom mansion. Even though his plans may have been grand, your expectations and needs rested on the three-bedroom. With such an extravagant design, to fill the house with furnishings would stretch your budget and go far beyond your capabilities.

Handling expectations is the major battle families face early in recovery. Hopefully, you now view this process through a broader perspective, which allows for more realistic expectations. Family members must form an idea of building that aligns with the other members involved. This helps ensure they are working toward the same blueprint. If expectations are too high on either side, disappointment and failure will surely arise. The family will find themselves unable to live up to the new goal. Discouragement and temptation to give up often follow.

These expectations revolve around daily schedules, recovery activities, family availability, goal setting, spiritual needs, emotional needs and simply the awkwardness of changing roles and responsibilities (see the Family Plan on page 154).

While planning offers a goal, flexibility is required of all involved. And the planning cannot be wrought under one person's control or the family system will revert to the faulty centering we have already discussed. In fact, Jesus is the only One authorized to set the forces of change in motion; He is the General Contractor. But His work happens in the heart.

Most often, family members would prefer a list of exactly what to expect and what to do to make things right. However, the planning and expectations that are set can't have specific how-to lists because the heart and healing are involved and everyone will be in their own stage of construction. Any fixing, manipulation, control or forced behavior usually causes tension, division and often self-protection. Family members are then prone to resort to the comfort of their adaptive roles (see Chapter 6).

It must be understood that things won't be perfect immediately. There may be days when rebuilding is clear and attitudes are healthy. There may be other days when negative mentalities seem more prevalent than anything new. Sometimes it can feel like three steps forward and two steps back. *Don't give up!* Construction sites are messy, and mentalities run deep. This is to be expected.

However, there can be expectations about sobriety that are clear and set apart. Expectations about other major behavioral issues can also be expressed. For example, if an addict also had a pornography addiction, that behavior can be considered just as unacceptable as substance use.

It's entirely common for an addict to switch addictions in the beginning phases of recovery. This may include food, sugar, work, exercise, codependency and more. The mentality of addiction has to be transformed gradually by the Holy Spirit. For an addict, this is a journey. Nonthreatening patterns of compulsive behavior may need to be granted allowances (for example, food, exercise, work). But inappropriate behaviors, such as sex addiction, should not be allowable. They threaten intimacy, respect and closeness; thus, they are never acceptable.

Boundaries in Responsibility

If you recall, in the book of Nehemiah families were assigned gates to fix. These gates were extremely important in the building process—while the wall was being established, the gates were the link to the outside world. They were also the most vulnerable to threats.

Like Nehemiah, family members must sit before their own "gates" and learn to secure their own part of the family system. The moment they leave their post and jump to help fix someone else's gate, they leave their own portion neglected. They also threaten the building process since unsolicited help will feel like control and may stir up conflict.

Therefore, as with an actual construction site, it's imperative to follow the overall plans, then work to secure each part. If your job is plumbing, then you aren't authorized to do electrical work. Family members are qualified by God to do a designated part. Responsibilities may overlap when necessary, but they should align in a fair and reasonable way as God intended. If that's not possible and a family member has needs that other members can't fill, that member needs to build an even stronger recovery and church community base.

Preparing for Conflict

The gate building in Nehemiah was extremely conflict-oriented because outside threats were constantly looming. Until those walls and gates were secure, the city remained vulnerable. In the same manner, even as the family attempts to rebuild, there will be many ways the enemy would like to come and disrupt the plans. The family can easily lose focus and revert to survival and adaptive roles, thus being unable to build something new. This focus and perseverance can be done only through helpful support that leads to God-dependency.

When People Fail

The truth is, the family will struggle to maintain a new goal and invariably fail in various ways. This will happen as controlling mentalities, disrespect, lack of submission, unhealthy emotions and other unhealthy behaviors manifest. That's why the most important ingredient in family planning is to have an understanding of grace. *Grace isn't about getting the job done right, but it is about understanding that most of the time we are incapable of doing it right.* Grace is a power source, but it is also a covering. Grace doesn't rely on human strength; it relies on the resources of God. Furthermore, it understands that failure is part of the journey and that grace can overcome those shortcomings and swallow up sinful mentalities that continue to linger. *Grace learns to find strength in weakness.*

We must come to understand how strong, capable and loving our God is and how weak, incapable and *un*able we are apart from Him. Yet through the empowerment of grace, we can do all things. God doesn't rescue us from challenges, but as we walk with Him, we become equipped and strengthened. If He just rescued us from everything, we'd never mature, grow and learn how to handle life in a healthy way. When we mess up, He stands close by to instruct, teach and work to make it right. He wants to bring this formula into the family system so everyone can walk with this awareness and level of humility.

As we mentioned already, God's grace doesn't allow sin; rather it covers it. The family will need to learn to let people fail to a degree and trust that Jesus will be able to deal with weaknesses. These are typically issues of the heart. However, if that failure brings toxic contaminants into the home and disrupts the building process, the other members most certainly have the right to enforce guidelines and consequences.

Relapse Planning

In all the conversation about building, it is essential to have a contingency plan should relapse in substance use (or toxic behaviors such as pornography) occur. This plan may not need to be implemented and prayerfully won't have to be. Instead, it offers a mode of storm prevention if the site comes under the attack of active addiction. The family has every right to protect the rebuilding process, yet that protection must remain under God's jurisdiction and not the faulty methods of adaption that took place in Chapter 6. Prayerfully, your family won't have to face this difficulty. But because relapse is common, it is a necessary step in planning.

Sometimes relapse is part of the journey toward long-term sobriety and recovery. Therefore, it doesn't have to be an all-or-nothing experience. Relapse doesn't have to last nor does it need to throw the family back into an addiction-centered formation.

By understanding that addiction steals the addict's life, the family can decide how to love the addict by hating and refusing addiction. If the addict truly wants freedom, they will agree to this. However, if the addict is resisting recovery, there is a good chance affection for the drugs or alcohol remains and they will resist creating a plan. Also, addicts fear control by family members and may perceive planning as a tool of control. That's why this process must be done in a respectful manner for everyone involved.

There is nothing a family member can do to prevent an addict from using. However, the family can establish an environment that will make that choice intolerable. It must be noted that *relapse isn't just the drug or alcohol—it's a mind-set.* Addicts typically pick up the substance after their mind becomes immersed in a thought system justifying its enticement. Addicts become obsessed with the idea of using before taking a drink or hit. Like a forbidden lover, they draw illicit plans on how and when to use again. In reality, they are back to medicating pain or trying to attain pleasure in a faulty way. They are trusting a counterfeit method to provide peace and joy. Therefore, true relapse prevention relates to the affections of the heart. The real remedy is securing affection for Jesus and being driven by His desires.

Symptoms of Relapse

Families can begin to see the obvious signs of relapse. Usually the addict's behavior will change. There may be long extensions of absence or complete departure for days on end. In recovery, we call this *going out.* Drug addicts tend to reconnect with an entire drug-use culture when relapse occurs.

When a family has spent resources and invested their hearts into the desire for sobriety, relapse can be infuriating. It can also be emotionally exhausting and provoke feelings of hopelessness. *However, relapse doesn't have to be the end.* In some cases, betrayal can be so intense that deeper long-term damage will occur. Each family needs to decide how to ultimately deal with a relapse. These principles were reviewed extensively in Chapter 7.

Even if relapse can be a learning experience for the addict, one thing *must* be part of that lesson: painful consequences. The only motivation for an addict to stop using is to see the reality of what it does. Being dropped back into the cycle of addiction must be uncomfortable. If the family reverts to survival living, they will return to the system that first allowed the addiction. In some ways, *this toxic-but-familiar system may be comfortable—and that's a temptation to be resisted.*

All relapse requires new intervention followed by a new recovery plan. An addict cannot simply have one drink or one hit and then go back to life as normal. The dynamics are set in motion and without a strong program, the result will be full-blown using.

It must be understood that *an addict should not participate in any addictive agents.* A heroin addict may convince the family that alcohol is okay. But heroin wasn't really the problem—the

Addiction & Recovery

Addictive Behaviors :

The need to blame
The stronghold of denial
Emotional and mental manipulation ("head games")
Manifestation of anger (through words or violence)
Chronic lying
Defensiveness
Immoral behaviors (cheating, stealing, sexual, etc.)
Secretiveness
Isolation
Unavailability
Bondage (no longer a choice to use drugs/alcohol)

Addiction Can be Disrupted When:

Family and friends set consequences for behavior
Addict is forced to feel ramifications of bad choices
Addict deals with overwhelming loss - nowhere to turn
Addict faces the potential of a marriage loss
Addict faces the potential of a job loss
Addict faces serious health problems
Addict faces serious criminal and legal problems
Addict has a spiritual encounter - conviction by the Holy Spirit

BOTTOMING OUT = BROKENNESS

Leads to repentance
Which leads to recovery

The Recovery Process

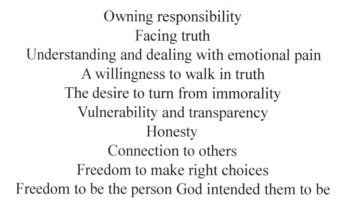

Owning responsibility
Facing truth
Understanding and dealing with emotional pain
A willingness to walk in truth
The desire to turn from immorality
Vulnerability and transparency
Honesty
Connection to others
Freedom to make right choices
Freedom to be the person God intended them to be

The Process Involves:

Surrender (Step 1)
Hope (Step 2)
A spiritual awakening (Step 3)
Time to sift and sort through emotional and spiritual issues
Emotional and spiritual maturity
Support from others going through the same thing
Grace - from God, self and others
The separation of behaviors from core identity
Forgiveness - giving and receiving
Embracing identity in Jesus Christ

Recovery Is Interrupted When:

Substance is reintroduced to system (immediate affect)
Stop working a program (gradual or immediate)
Focus switches to new or difficult relationship (gradual or immediate)
Return to willful immoral lifestyle (gradual or immediate)
Stop being open, honest and transparent (gradual)
Allow bitterness and resentments into heart (gradual)

Leads back to

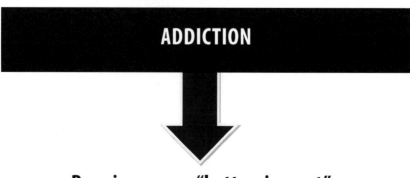

ADDICTION

Requires a new "bottoming out"

mind-set of addiction was. Therefore, alcohol cannot only become a physical dependency but it can also keep the addict unable to recover and deal with rooted issues.

How the family responds to relapse will greatly impact the addict. Through a relapse plan, some preplanned actions steps can be taken. These include the following:

- Discussion of the living situation (if applicable) if the addict uses
- Financial support
- Any other areas that have been brought to the surface

The family's goal will be not to enable when offering the addict freedom from control and the ability to make choices. The addict's need is to come to their senses and learn once and for all that addiction will destroy them—and that the advantages of sobriety far outweigh any advantages a high could bring.

Drug Testing

If a relapse is not obvious but there is a clear pattern of behavior changes, it is a fair request that the family agree upon drug testing. There is a variety of options available on the market, and healthcare and treatment facilities that can assist with this.

However, if families hover over the addict with drug tests readily available, control will make the addict feel threatened. The family should not be authorized to have a drug test in hand at every given moment. However, a fair and reasonable agreement can be decided through family planning that can assure the family of sobriety if one of the following is happening:

- Long absences from the home occur without any justifiable excuse.
- Anger, unhealthy emotions and isolation become predominant and extend for weeks on end.
- Physical symptoms are present that indicate relapse correlating to the drug itself.
- Recovery activities cease.

Ideally, the addict in sobriety will see addiction as a deadly condition and agree that these signs may indicate the disease has come to life. In the Family Plan, the addict can help secure sobriety by warning the family of what a relapse might entail and asking the family to hold him or her accountable if or when it occurs. Addicts who are using and in full-blown addiction will lie and be manipulative. If testing has been agreed upon, it must be understood not every doctor's office will be a good place to do this. That's because the drug addict will try every tactic possible to produce a clean test. This may include consuming something before the test, hiding urine somewhere inside clothing or bags or other sneaky tactics. Thus, drug testing should be done at a location (or at home) that will include monitoring of the specimen being produced. Drug and alcohol treatment facilities and some medical clinics normally offer these services.

Addiction and Recovery

Families must learn addiction and recovery require two separate responses. When in recovery, the addict will be going through a transformation process in which God touches and captivates the heart. When in addiction, addicts will be going through a process of inner death—in which they are separated from Him and experience the negative consequences of the addiction cycle. By learning both cycles have different needs and requirements, family members can learn to embrace their own parts accordingly. To demonstrate this, please review the charts on pages 145 and 146. These will highlight the two dynamics that addiction and recovery cause. In family planning, it must be understood that two plans will be used:

1. Intervention Plan: This is the actual plan of intervention as discussed in Chapter 7.
2. Recovery plan: This must be an actual plan based on recovery principles (we will cover this plan in this chapter).

Writing a Family Plan

The end of this chapter contains a resource to assist in family planning. How or when this can be used depends on individual circumstances. You cannot force planning to occur. If you are dealing with an addict who doesn't want accountability or structure in recovery, you may need to create your own boundaries to deal with this. Thus, you will work on your own plan apart from the addict. If you are afraid or skeptical of involvement in this process because of past hurts, you shouldn't be manipulated to fill this out. You do have a choice. Just understand this isn't to hurt or favor one side over the other. It's to initiate a difficult and sometimes painful dialogue. The real purpose is to openly discuss and plan with healthy expectations. As with anything, you can always customize and adapt this to your own needs

A plan in itself can't implement change, and it certainly can't affect the heart directly. An external plan can't affect internal needs. However, it acts as a source of understanding and guidance for everyone involved. If you don't have a facilitator, such as a counselor or sponsor, to assist in this process, be sure you have read the material completely and have an understanding of what's involved. You may want to join some recovery groups right away to help you see other people's perspective of similar situations. There is nothing more difficult than feeling you are facing something alone, and there is nothing more comforting than realizing others are going through the same thing. The truth is that you are not alone. There are millions of other family members in your shoes facing these tough decisions.

It is understandable not to want to be forced to make decisions if you still feel confused. But don't let that stop you from gaining the tools of healthy family planning. It is a vital and key ingredient for everyone involved.

This plan is only for the family who enters into the mode of recovery. When active addiction occurs, this plan is no longer effective. Instead, families must prepare to write and plan on intervention and personal boundaries.

As with everything, you can *always* seek the assistance of the Holy Spirit. You don't have to walk this alone. It's also critical to find human beings (preferably who understand redemption in Jesus Christ) to help you on this journey.

For the Spouse

This plan reflects the intimate nature of the relationship between a husband and wife. The marriage covenant is the most influential and affected relationship in the addiction cycle. It's also the relationship that most needs healing to endure the storm of addiction.

The initial goal of planning is to set up safe ground rules that allow each side to focus on their own healing within proper expectations. It is critical that individual roles be discussed at the beginning because these roles have often been extremely confused in the addiction cycle. However, in being able to articulate those roles, there must be an understanding that the relationship itself needs time to mend. In other words, the perfect mate won't magically pop out overnight! Damage has been done, hurt needs to be processed and God's healing must be given time to take effect. If either spouse pressures the other to deal with the relationship itself, the relationship may become jeopardized. This pressure can stimulate an environment of emotional intensity and cause unhealthy defense mechanisms to be used. Relapse is always the responsibility of the addict; however, when the environment contains pressure and a chronic sense of failure, relapse is prone to occur.

The need for *individual* recovery is as simple as a physical building needing reconstruction after it has been destroyed. There are distinct, individual steps involved in the process of rebuilding. First, the debris must be removed. Then, a new *foundation* must be established. This must happen before the walls and roof can be erected, making the construction begin to resemble a home.

The foundation of a marriage must have a relationship with Jesus as the priority—and His ministry to *each individual* must be a priority as well. If one spouse isn't in relationship with Him, there is a need to secure wisdom and direction to deal with the nature of the imbalance. This is something any married couple faces when one receives Christ but the other does not. The Bible tells us marriage is so sacred, God desires we honor the spouse and pray that he or she will come to know Jesus. However, this imbalance does put pressure on the relationship. If the addict is the spouse who is not a Christian, the recovery community can still effectively lead him or her to Christ. Don't lose hope! Keep praying!

When both the addict and spouse are working a recovery program, there may be a season of what seems like detachment. It can feel as though—in being asked to focus on their individual issues—the spousal relationship is placed on hold. But during this period, mutual prayer, communication and goal setting can be done. The unhealthy bond and old patterns of adaptation must be severed—*but not to destroy the relationship*. Rather, it's to *reset* the relationship.

We can compare the relationship to a physical bone that has been broken but not properly cared for in the healing process. If the broken bone isn't properly set, it will heal incorrectly. Various damaging effects will result including infection, disability of the bone and arthritis. In some cases, the bone must actually be broken again so it can realign and heal properly.

The first stage of relationship recovery can seem painful because of the "re-breaking" that must be done to remove the unhealthy ways the relationship had been "set." As with the bone that was improperly fused together, that breaking apart may *feel* like an end but it is often God's new beginning! He's not trying to destroy the relationship—He seeks to restore it. But to access restoration, He first needs to rid the residue and the dysfunction that caused it to work incorrectly in the first place. *This is what individual recovery seeks to resolve.* But from there, the relationship has the opportunity to heal for God's purposes and plans.

Spouses often want specifics on how long it takes life to become normal. And there is simply no way to measure this because of the many variables involved. It will take however long it takes and be whatever it needs to be. Setting specifics on this will usher in deep disappointment when things don't move as quickly as expected. The process is very reflective of the two individuals' personal needs. Some couples have received a grand intervention with their entire marriages falling into place rather quickly. But this is not the norm. Most couples have gradually and slowly implemented change and still struggle with a variety of relationship issues. But over time, wonderful relationships can be formed.

Marriages fail in the recovery phase when healthy communication doesn't occur. When both sides continue to blame, criticize, judge and expect the other to do all the changing, there will be a major breakdown. At the same time, active addiction may also end the relationship. This is not God's desire, and it shouldn't be considered an option unless the situation is so intolerable there is no other choice. Because of this, sobriety must first take center stage. Everything will fall apart without sobriety—leaving no marriage to work on if the addict is using.

While a spouse can offer much input and assist in details in the planning process, they do not have a license to control. Control will always be the enemy of all forms of healing and redemption. In fact, the entire planning process is designed to begin a healthy conversation with respect and thoughtful consideration of each other's needs.

A Prayer for the Spouse

Father,

Help me sift and sort through the rubbish of the storm to determine what I need to release. Give me hope and perseverance that recovery is about cleansing and preparing us to make marriage as You intended. Help us through the seasons of transition. We ask for your abundant grace to be our power and strength. Show me how and where I need to own my part. Give me supernatural love for my spouse so I can see him or her as You do.

In Jesus' name, amen.

A Note to Parents of Adult Children

As much as the marriage relationship undergoes significant upheaval, the situation parents face is equally difficult. A parent has a unique position as caregiver to that child even when he or she has become an adult. So much time and effort had been invested in overseeing, caring for and seeking to help that child mature. There is naturally a sense of responsibility for that child's needs.

Most of us can identify with the levels of detachment that occur as a child matures. From their first steps, to the entrance to kindergarten, through the high school years, to marriage (if applicable), we are continually called to decrease our parental role and allow our children to increase ownership of their lives.

In addiction, this process gets stunted. Sometimes the adult child takes on characteristics that keep them in a childlike form. And the parents naturally continue to respond as if the adult child needs oversight. However, in truth, the addict needs to grow up and take ownership of life choices. This may have to occur gradually as opposed to immediately, but it will need to occur.

The parents of an adult addict in recovery must take this season as seriously as a graduation to life ceremony. Recovery is about maturing, growing up and moving on. To illustrate this need, consider the caterpillar. It engages in the metamorphosis process as it leaves the youth of being a caterpillar to begin the final destination of becoming a butterfly. To make this transition, the butterfly must first prepare accordingly. The butterfly must squeeze and push its wings out of the cramped space of the chrysalis meticulously, slowly and perhaps even painfully. If a well-meaning human observed this struggle and kindly clipped the chrysalis open before the strengthening exercise, disaster would occur. The wings would not fully develop and the butterfly would not be strong enough to fly. In fact, the butterfly would eventually perish.

This graduation to flight is an accurate picture of a parent and child in the dynamic of addiction. The key for the addict is to learn how to take on wings and make right choices. At times, this means the addict will be squeezed and pressured through difficulties. Although it's tempting to continue to nurture and help the addict in every need, perseverance, strength, character and healthy coping skills must be developed. It's tempting to prevent the pain of those struggles, but they may be the very things that will lead the addict into the necessary strength to bring them to their God-desired destiny.

No matter how it may be described, the parents' struggle can't be diminished nor the pain invalidated. A personal recovery program is encouraged for the parents to unload the burden of responsibility and to learn better ways to cope. Parents often carry incredible guilt and shame for their child's addiction. This can happen especially if that child was exposed to a difficult upbringing. Then the parents carry two burdens: a painful past and the reality of their child's struggle. Personal recovery will help a parent work through this.

It must be understood that the family-planning process between an adult child in recovery and a parent must be an *adult* discussion. It doesn't matter if the addict has been childish in behavior; the addict needs to graduate into adulthood.

All planning done with parents, therefore, should be based on mutual respect, not on parental authority. The parent can't own responsibility for the addict. Also, continuing to support the addict as one would a dependent child is destructive for everyone. Certainly, a level of assistance may be necessary, but it shouldn't remain dependency based. All assistance an adult child receives should be for the sole purpose of eventually being able to manage their life without that assistance. In others words, it's just a hand up, not a lifestyle.

A parent's deepest need, therefore, is to learn how to love and how to release. If this is a personal struggle, you are not alone. That's why finding a community of other parents on the same journey will be an incredible gift.

A Parent's Prayer
Dear Lord,
Thank you for the honor of parenting. I know I didn't do it perfectly, but You know that my

intentions were good. I ask that You release me from any guilt or shame I have been carrying because of _____'s addiction. I realize the weight of that needs to be removed for my own healing process to occur. I recognize this is the season of release. I need to let go and give _____ to You. _____ is Your child now or will hopefully be in the future. I want to do my part to support _____ to be the person You created him or her to be. Meanwhile, help me formulate the practical steps of that release. Show me where to help and where to let go.

In Jesus' name, amen.

Making a Pledge

In the book of Nehemiah and throughout the Old Testament, God's people dedicated completed construction sites to the Lord. This happened when the temple was rebuilt and when the walls of Jerusalem were reestablished. Dedicating the *family's* rebuilding project to the Lord is a sacred act. God doesn't take such a pledge lightly. Therefore, it's something that can't be imposed or just expected. If the family members can mutually *agree* on a plan and *desire* to sign the pledge included in this chapter, it is a form of making a covenant with the Lord. This is not an *emotional* transaction; it is a *spiritual* transaction. Not only does it bring honor to the Lord, but it also removes authority from the addict-centered family and places it onto Him. A decision to leave the old and let God bring forth the new must be induced by the Holy Spirit.

Affecting the World

Addiction doesn't affect only the immediate people in the family system. Addiction affects the entire community, the body of Christ and future generations. How we choose to respond to addiction is an individual mandate. When God can raise one or all family members out of the debris of addiction and bring answers, He can bring hope to a larger audience. There is a world hurting and waiting to see if the God of the Bible we claim is real. Step 12 in the 12-step program revolves around bringing the message of freedom to others.

Right now, a testimony in and of itself isn't the goal. Authentic solution and recovery must first be received in order to be offered. But your response to the promises and purposes of God has many more ramifications than you can even imagine.

Addiction most likely wasn't in your life plan. It wasn't something you signed up for, wanted or even thought you'd have to deal with. But it happened—to you and millions and millions of other family members. As horrible as it is, you don't have to remain the victim of the storm site when you have the Author of Redemption working on your behalf. The God of the Bible redeems. The God of the Bible raises people up and rebuilds in the very places the enemy intended to destroy. This is your opportunity to know Him, to respond to His call and to make His power known around you. Like Nehemiah, you can be the generation that sees the wall rebuilt in your own family. Don't settle for second best. Don't let the lies of the enemy speak louder than the truth of God. You matter to God. He is bigger, and He is able.

This is what the Word implores us:

> "Today I have given you the choice between life and death, between blessings and curses. Now I call on heaven and earth to witness the choice you make.

Oh, that you would choose life, so that you and your descendants might live!" (Deuteronomy 30:19)

A Prayer of Pledge When My Family Isn't Ready

Lord,

I establish a covenant with You even if I can't pursue the restoration of my family right now. I believe that You can clean up my own storm site and bring forth purpose and blessing despite what those around me do. Bring me into the healing process and allow me to be free to walk in identity and purpose. I commit to my own gate of rebuilding. I believe You are bigger than the threats that will assault me. I trust You for the task of rebuilding. I pray that You give me a holy burden like Nehemiah to plead and beg for the restoration of my family. Remind me of the rebuilding of those ancient walls when I see my own circumstances as hopeless. They are not hopeless—not when You are able to work!

In Jesus' name, amen.

A Prayer When the Family Is Ready to Mutually Seek Planning

Father,

We offer to You our home and our hearts. We lay down our own agenda and pick up Your leadership. We ask that You would lead us through our discussion of planning. Give us compassion and concern for each other. Help us to not only look after our own needs—but also to look upon them. Allow no manipulation or control to set the parameters of this conversation. May it be covered and anointed by Your Holy Spirit. Give us teachable and reachable hearts to be humble, honest and vulnerable. Allow us to *own* our personal responsibilities and be accountable rather than driven to blame. Allow us to honor You and prepare for You to rebuild our lives. Make us a family that can symbolize Your power and glory. When conflicts hit, remind us of Nehemiah and the endurance he displayed because he knew his God. May we trust You in the same manner. May we know You are faithful to complete that which You began.

In Jesus' name, amen.

FAMILY RECOVERY PLAN

"Today I have given you the choice between life and death, between blessings and curses. Now I call on heaven and earth to witness the choice you make. Oh, that you would choose life, so that you and your descendants might live!" (Deuteronomy 30:19)

ADDICTS IN RECOVERY

I am sharing the following information with you regarding my support plans.

Meeting and Support

- ☐ I will secure a sponsor and work closely with him or her to transition to a life of sobriety.
- ☐ I will need to attend _____ meetings a week. I need your support.
- ☐ I will need to add these additional things to my week to assure I can remain sober:

_____

_____

_____

_____

Living Situation: (☐ Check here if N/A):

I need to be physically absent from drugs and alcohol. I am concerned about triggers and potential snares in my recovery process. I'd like to discuss our housing situation (if applicable).

The home I'm returning to will contain:

- ☐ Alcohol use.
- ☐ Drug use.
- ☐ Prescription meds.

I feel that I:

- ☐ Can work with this.
- ☐ Cannot work with this.

I have decided I will need to live at (home, sober living house, etc.):

_____

- • This plan is: ☐ permanent ☐ temporary
- • If temporary, I plan to live here for (length of time): _____
- • These plans may change under these conditions:
    - ☐ I later realize it is an environment where I am not safe and cannot remain sober.
    - ☐ If I relapse, I may need another setting.

Emotional Needs:

I am dealing with emotional issues that are new and raw. I need you to understand that my emotions are still not always stable. Please allow me space and time. To help honor and facilitate both sides of the emotional healing process, I am asking you to understand this. I would like to agree on some set parameters.

- Please allow me to deal with emotions without trying to change my emotions.
- Please understand I can't handle all the emotional problems we have in our relationship at one time.
- When emotional issues arise and bring strain, please let me work through my recovery plan to deal with them.
- _____
_____
_____
_____
- _____
_____
_____
_____

Choices:

I need to make decisions based on God's direction. I will seek to respect my family and others when I make these decisions. I need to learn the benefit or consequences of my choices. I ask that you please allow me the space to make these choices. At the same time, I wish to respect your right to make choices. I would like to cease any control I used in our relationship to get what I wanted.

Responsibility:

I have been irresponsible as the _____ of our family. These are some of the ways I realize I wasn't available:

_____
_____
_____
_____

I realize that I hurt everyone as a result. I want to learn to regain your trust and be placed in this position. This includes the following:

_____
_____
_____
_____

I agree to work with you through a method of allowing me back into my role. I also understand that if I do something irresponsible, there may need to consequences. I feel this should happen whether or not addiction is present. This includes the following:

_____
_____
_____

Spiritual Needs:

I have given my life to the Lord. I have experienced change, but I will not be perfect. Please respect my need to grow and mature in the Lord. I will be participating in some of the following:

- ☐ Attend church _____.
- ☐ Receive spiritual mentoring.
- ☐ Do daily devotions privately.
- ☐ Attend Bible study _____.
- ☐ Serve in the body of Christ _____.

Finances:

Respond to only those that apply:

- ☐ I am dependent on my family financially.
- ☐ I am not dependent on the family for finances.
- ☐ I will fulfill my own role to assist the family financially. If I'm in the position of being supported, I will honor your support. (Please note: A husband still is financially responsible for the family even if he is not the breadwinner.)
- ☐ If I need to find employment, I am committed to looking at any and all options.
- ☐ I am committed to spending _____ hours a day seeking a job.
- ☐ If I do not actively seek employment, I understand that I am a financial burden on my family. This may strain the family and cause boundaries to be implemented. I agree to be held accountable to do what I can, but please allow me to do this on my own. I need your support, but I need to take responsibility for these decisions.
- ☐ I agree to _____ (husband, wife, etc.) making the primary financial decisions.
- ☐ If I am responsible for this position, I agree my decision making may need to be surrendered if a relapse should occur.
- ☐ I agree to stop using my role wrongfully to gain finances from you.

Relapse:

I believe I will not relapse or ever have to implement this. However, for our protection, I would like to offer this relapse plan. Please remember, *I am not my addiction*. If I relapse, I will come under a system that hurts you and me. Therefore, I give you permission to hold me accountable but not control my ability to make choices.

My biggest symptoms of relapse include the following:

_____

_____

_____

_____

When those symptoms are obvious, I agree to submit to drug testing. The method of this test should be: _____.

When in relapse, I agree that you can implement the plan we have agreed on. I understand that my family cares about my well-being and wants me to be sober. Therefore, I will agree to the following actions if relapse occurs:

_____

_____

_____

_____

Goals:

I would like to share with you my goals for my life and our family (this is only done if mutually agreed upon. Some families would rather not share these at this point. Also, this is intended for a married couple as opposed to a parent/adult child).

ONE WEEK
Individual:

_____

_____

_____

_____

Family:

_____

_____

_____

_____

ONE MONTH
Individual:

_____

_____

_____

_____

Family:

_____

_____

_____

_____

SIX MONTHS
Individual:

_____

_____
_____
_____

Family:

_____
_____
_____
_____

1 YEAR
Individual:

_____
_____
_____
_____

Family:

_____
_____
_____

Confession and Repentance:
Receiving Forgiveness
I am working through the issues of my heart. I seek to ask you to forgive me for wrongs I have done against you. I confess this to you:

- ☐ I am still processing through this and am not ready to have a discussion right now.
- ☐ I am ready to confess my wrongs to you.

_____
_____
_____
_____
_____
_____
_____
_____

Offering Forgiveness:
I may need to forgive you for something that hurt me in our relationship.

- ☐ I am still processing through this and am not ready to have a discussion right now.
- ☐ I am ready to forgive you and release you, but will not accept this behavior in the future.

Over time, I want our relationship to be:

_____
_____
_____
_____
_____
_____
_____
_____
_____

Affirmation

I want to tell you the positive things about you and how much I appreciate these things about you:

_____
_____
_____
_____
_____
_____
_____
_____
_____
_____

FAMILY MEMBERS IN RECOVERY

I want to communicate my recovery plans with you. I am seeking to be supported outside our family system so I can adjust to a life with your sobriety and protect against reentering the cycle.

Meeting and Support:
- ☐ N/A - I won't be sharing this
- ☐ I will secure a sponsor and work closely with him or her to transition to learning how to live with you sober.
- ☐ I will need to attend _____ meetings a week. I need your support.
- ☐ I will need to add these additional things to my week to assure I can support you and myself during this change.

_____
_____
_____
_____

Our Living Situation: (☐ Check here if n/a)

☐ I no longer wish to live with addiction in my home. I am supporting your recovery, but I no longer want to participate in active addiction. For you to return home, I am asking for the following:

- o Your sobriety.
- o Your willingness to test when warning signs are clearly present.
- o Your willingness to live in sober housing if you are not stable enough to live here.

This criteria includes:

_____
_____
_____

☐ I would like to continue to allow some substance in our home. This includes the following:

_____.

Emotional Needs:

I have been holding onto many of the emotional needs of our family or have been trying to avoid them altogether. While you work out your recovery, I also need to work through mine.

☐ Please understand I have been hurt; please be sensitive to my pain. I cannot necessarily snap out of it, but I am committed to work through my own recovery process (if applicable).

☐ Please be sensitive to my emotional needs that have been unmet. I understand you won't be able to fix my needs and that you have to concentrate on your own, but it is still helpful to know that you are supportive.

- _____
_____
_____
- _____
_____
_____
_____

Responsibility:

I have been overcompensating in the following ways to deal with your addiction:

_____
_____
_____
_____

I am ready to give back the responsibilities that belong to you. These include the following:

_____

_____

_____

_____

Finances (Applicable):

Because you support me financially, I feel that it is fair that we share accountability. I would like to request the following:

_____

_____

_____

_____

I have supported you financially, and these are my concerns:

_____

_____

_____

_____

I feel changes need to be made in the following area(s):

_____

_____

_____

_____

Relapse Agreement:

I understand that you are not your addiction. I agree to have a relapse plan in place so I can love you but not allow your addiction. This plan will be designed with absolutely *no tolerance* to any substance use.

I agree to these steps in relapse:

- ☐ If living in our home, the following action will occur: _____

  _____

- ☐ We will not support you financially through a relapse if you cannot support yourself.
- ☐ We will not enable you in any way in a relapse.
- ☐ To create an environment for you to return and be reconciled with us, we want to see this action occur:

  _____

  _____

Goals:

I would like to share with you my goals for my life and our family. (This is only done if mutually agreed upon. Some families would rather not share these at this point. Also, this is relevant for married couples, it would not be applicable for adult children and their parents).

ONE WEEK
Individual:

_____
_____
_____
_____

Family:

_____
_____
_____
_____

ONE MONTH
Individual:

_____
_____
_____
_____

Family:

_____
_____
_____
_____

SIX MONTHS
Individual:

_____
_____
_____
_____

Family:

_____
_____
_____
_____

1 YEAR
Individual:

_____

_____
_____
_____

Family:

_____
_____
_____

My Pledge of Giving and Receiving Forgiveness
Offering Forgiveness
I am working to offer you forgiveness. I may need time. While I want to, I need untangle from it and see this accurately.

- ☐ I am ready to forgive you (not recommended unless there has been recovery and the family member understands the hurt. Forgiveness can be misunderstood).
- ☐ I would like to wait and continue to work through this. I am committed to forgive.
- ☐ I am angry right now, I need to not discuss this right now.

Receiving Forgiveness
I realize that while I feel I was hurt and betrayed, I may have participated in some unhealthy behaviors.

- ☐ I am ready to confess my wrongs to you.
- ☐ I would like to wait and continue to work through this.

_____
_____
_____
_____

Over time, I want our relationship to be:

_____
_____
_____
_____

Affirmation
I want to tell you the positive things about you and how much I appreciate these things about you:

_____
_____
_____
_____

_____

_____

_____

_____

_____

A Pledge

I dedicate this plan unto the Lord, on this day _____ of

_____, _____.

Addict Signature:

_____

Family Signature:

_____

Family Signature:

_____

A Pledge

Today I have given you the choice between life and death, between blessings and curses. Now I call on heaven and earth to witness the choice you make. Oh, that you would choose life, so that you and your descendants might live – Deuteronomy 30:19

❖ *We give our family to God. We make Him the Head and the Centering Point of everything we are and will become.*

❖ *We trust God with the task of dealing with our heart issues. We give Him the rightful position of being our Healer, Redeemer, Savior, Heart Changer, Transformer and Guide.*

❖ *We believe no matter the condition of our family, God is powerful and big enough to restore it to its God-given design.*

❖ *We release our efforts to control our own lives and each other. We recognize that only God is worthy of control.*

❖ *We make love the priority of our lives and our relationships. We believe everything else is fruitless if love isn't present.*

❖ *We realize we can't love without recognizing that God first loved us and gives us the ability to love each other. Instead of pressuring each other to love, we commit to love God first in our hearts.*

❖ *We respect and honor each other's needs to go through recovery. We commit to avoiding expectations that are unreasonable or unfair.*

❖ *We commit to our own recovery process so we can stay in the light and be free on the inside.*

❖ *We release our adaptive roles and the methods we used to survive. We ask for grace to help us make those transitions in a positive way.*

❖ *We commit to learning our God-given roles and responsibilities and pledge to work them out on a daily basis.*

❖ *We recognize that only grace empowers us, and we will all fall short. We give allowances for each other's weaknesses.*

❖ *We will not allow substance addiction, deep immorality or other addictive influences to center our home. We ask that You place spiritual protection around our home and hearts.*

❖ *We ask that any demonic influence be commanded to leave and that angels would be sent to guard our home. We believe that Your Spirit can cover each of us individually.*

❖ *We submit to the conviction of Your Holy Spirit to deal with our hearts and tell us when we have something that needs to be changed. Keep us in the light—keep our hearts tender.*

❖ *We agree to confess our sins to each other and admit our weaknesses rather than cover them. We will honor each other's vulnerability.*

❖ *We will promote words that encourage and build up in our home.*

Dedication to Rebuild

THIS CERTIFICATE RECOGNIZES THAT OUR FAMILY

_____

Is dedicated to move beyond the storm of addiction and move into the life

God intended on this _____ *of* _____ .

IN THE PRESENCE OF

_____

_____
Family Member

_____
Family Member

_____
Family Member

"Today I have given you the choice between life and death, between blessings and curses. Now I call on heaven and earth to witness the choice you make. Oh, that you would choose life, so that you and your descendants might live!"

Resources

Free Workshops and Webinars

Join us live or via webinar to go chapter by chapter through
a teaching-led process of these books:

Christian Families in Recovery

*The Christian Codependence Recovery Workbook:
From Surviving to Significance*

A House that Grace Built

Sponsored by Spirit of Life Recovery

Please note: Besides the services and materials of New Life Spirit Recovery and Spirit of Life Recovery, we don't endorse the resources listed directly, but have found them useful in various ways. These are for your own further information, reading or study. Please use discretion in the content.

Treatment & Counseling

Professional substance addiction treatment and counseling
New Life Spirit Recovery
www.newlifespiritrecovery.com
866.543.3361

Professional codependence treatment and counseling
New Life Spirit Recovery
18652 Florida Street, Suite 200
Huntington Beach, CA 92648
www.newlifespiritrecovery.com
866.543.3361

For referrals to local counseling services:
American Association of Christian Counselors
P.O. Box 739
Forest, VA 24551
800.526.8673
www.aacc.net

Hotline: 866.543.3363
(referral and services)

Meeting & Groups

Celebrate Recovery
Search locally
www.celebraterecovery.com

Al-Anon
Search locally
www.al-anon.alateen.org

Adult Children of Alcoholics
Search locally
adultchildren.org

Codependents Anonoymous
Search locally via website
www.coda.org

Websites

Codependent Resources
www.christiancodependence.org

Focus on the Family
Parenting and information
on the family
www.focusonthefamily.com

Focus Ministries
Help for domestic abuse
www.focusministries1.org

Books

*The Christian Codependence Workbook:
From Surviving to Significance*
by Stephanie Tucker

*A House that Grace Built: Moving
Beyond Codependence to
Embrace God's Design for Love,
Relationships & Wholeness*
By Stephanie Tucker

Families Where Grace is in Place
by Jeff VanVonderen

Freedom From Addiction
by Neil Anderson

A Hunger for Healing
by J. Keith Miller

Love Must Be Tough
by James Dobson

*Setting Boundaries with Your
Adult Children*
by Allison Bottke

Have questions?

Call our free resource line at 866.543.3361